EFFECTIVE NATURAL HOME REMEDIES FOR COMMON AILMENTS

Foods that heal

Kenneth Milkas

Kens Publishing

CONTENTS

INTRODUCTION

Are you or your loved one's frequently waiting outside the doctor's chamber for an ailing body?

Natural health remedies are having a serious moment on the wellness scene right now.

Frequently suffering from the illness of any sort is a clear indication of the fact that you have a weak immune system, and should not take that very lightly.
Medicines have side-effects, so frequently consuming them can also affect your health adversely and decrease life expectancy.

This book is collection of natural home remedies, if followed diligently, can certainly help you boost your immune system and prevent several common illnesses.

We rounded up few of the most common remedies here– but remember, if you're really worried, you should always see a doctor.

The advantage of using home remedies is, of course, that they're often low- to no-cost and they can quickly heal without a doctor appointment or an expensive trip to the pharmacy.

The age-old proverb "prevention is better than cure" is
has its base in cold, hard truth.

STOMACH ACIDITY

1. Basil Leaves

The soothing and carminative properties of basil leaves can give you instant relief from acidity. At the first sign of gas, eat a few basil leaves or boil 3-4 basil leaves in a cup of water and let it simmer for a few minutes. Sip on it frequently. This is one of the best home remedies for acidity.

2. Fennel

You can also "chew sauf after meals, to prevent stomach acidity", advises Nutritionist Anshul Jaibharat. "For its multitude of gastrointestinal benefits, fennel tea is sure to help the digestive tract be healthy and happy. The tea is considered very useful to help indigestion and b-loating because of the oils found in these seeds", according to Shilpa Arora ND, a renowned Health Practitioner, Nutritionist and certified Macrobiotic Health Coach.

3. Cinnamon

This humble spice works as a natural antacid for stomach acidity and can settle your stomach, by improving digestion and absorption. For relief, drink cinnamon tea to heal infections in the gastrointestinal tract. Cinnamon is a powerhouse of nutrients and loaded with health benefiting properties.

4. Buttermilk

Did you know that buttermilk is categorised as a sattvic food in Ayurveda? So, the next time you get acidity after eating a heavy or spicy meal, skip the antacid and drink a glass of chaas instead. Buttermilk contains lactic acid that normalizes acidity in the stomach. Sprinkle a dash of black pepper or 1 teaspoon of ground coriander leaves for best results.

5. Jaggery

Ever wondered why our elders finish a meal with gur? "Due to its high magnesium content, jaggery helps boost intestinal strength", says Dr. Manoj K. Ahuja, Fortis Hospital, New Delhi. It aids digestion and makes your digestive system more alkaline in nature, thus reducing stomach acidity. Suck on a small piece of gur after a meal, and reap the benefits. Since jaggery also helps maintain normal body temperature, cooling the stomach - experts recommend drinking Gur Sharbat (jaggery soaked in ice cold water) during the summer.

6. Cloves

Over the years, cloves have grabbed a prominent place in traditional Chinese medicine and Ayurveda to treat digestive disorders. Cloves are carminative in nature, thus preventing the formation of gas in the gastrointestinal tract. Add cloves while cooking foods like kidney beans or black gram that tend to cause flatulence. You can even eat crushed cloves and cardamom (mixed in equal amounts) to treat acidity, and get rid of bad breath (which often accompanies this problem).

7. Cumin Seeds

Cumin seeds work as a great acid neutralizer, aid digestion and relieve stomach pain. Slightly crush some roasted cumin seeds, stir it into a glass of water or steep one teaspoon of cumin seeds in a cup of boiled water and drink it after every meal.

8. Ginger

Beneath its knobbly exterior, ginger hides many health benefits. "Ginger has excellent digestive and anti-inflammatory properties", says Dr. Ahuja, Fortis Hospital. To help neutralize stomach acids, you can chew a slice of fresh ginger, or have a spoonful of ginger juice two-three times a day, or steep fresh ginger in a cup of boiling water and drink up.

9. Cold Milk

For those who are not lactose intolerant, milk can help stabilize gastric acids in the stomach. It is rich in calcium, which prevents the build-up of acid in the stomach. "All you need to do is drink a glass of cold milk the next time you suffer from acidity", suggests Nutritionist Anshul Jaibharat.

10. Apple Cider Vinegar

Very often, your acid reflux is in fact the result of too little stomach acid. That's where apple cider vinegar steps in. Simply mix 1-2 teaspoons of raw, unfiltered apple cider vinegar in a cup of water and drink it once or twice a day. You can also take a tablespoon of apple cider vinegar, and chase it with a glass of water.

11. Coconut Water

"When you drink coconut water, your body's pH acidic level turns alkaline", adds Dr. Ahuja, Fortis Hospital. It also helps produce mucous in your stomach, which protects the stomach from harmful effects of excessive acid production. Since it is rich in fibre, it aids digestion and prevents the re-occurrence of acidity.

12. Banana

When it comes to health benefiting properties, bananas hold much importance. Bananas contain natural ant-acids that can act as a buffer against acid reflux. This is the simplest home remedy for getting rid of acidity. Eat one banana every day to prevent discomfort.

So, if you ever happen to suffer from acidity, then bring these home remedies to your rescue.

ACNE

1. Apply Apple Cider Vinegar

Apple cider vinegar is made by fermenting apple cider, or the unfiltered juice from pressed apples.

Like other vinegars, it is known for its ability to fight many types of bacteria and viruses.

Apple cider vinegar contains several organic acids that have been shown to kill acnes.

In particular, succinic acid has been shown to suppress inflammation caused by P. acnes, which may prevent scarring.

Also, lactic acid has been shown to improve the appearance of acne scars.

What's more, apple cider vinegar may help dry up the excess oil that causes acne in the first place.

How to use it
   1. Mix 1part apple cider vinegar and 3 parts water

(use more water for sensitive skin).

2. After cleansing, gently apply the mixture to the skin using a cotton ball.

3. Let sit for 5–20 seconds, rinse with water and pat dry.

4. Repeat this process 1–2 times per day, as needed.

It is important to note that applying apple cider vinegar to your skin can cause burns and irritation, so it should always be used in small amounts and diluted with water.

SUMMARY

The organic acids in apple cider vinegar may help kill acne-causing bacteria and reduce the appearance of scars. Applying it to the skin may cause burns or irritation, so it should be used carefully.

2. Take A Zinc Supplement

Zinc is an essential nutrient that's important for cell growth, hormone production, metabolism and immune function.

It is also one of the most studied natural treatments for acne. Research shows that people with acne tend to have lower levels of zinc in their blood than those with clear skin.

Several studies have shown that taking zinc orally helps

reduce acne.

In one study, 48 acne patients were given oral zinc supplements three times per day. After eight weeks, 38 patients experienced an 80–100% reduction in acne.

The optimal dosage of zinc for acne has not been established, but several studies have shown a significant reduction of acne using 30–45 mg of elemental zinc per day.

Elemental zinc refers to the amount of zinc that's present in the compound. Zinc is available in many forms, and each one contains a different amount of elemental zinc.

Zinc oxide contains the highest amount of elemental zinc at 80%.

The recommended safe upper limit of zinc is 40 mg per day, so it is probably best to not exceed that amount unless under the supervision of a medical doctor. Taking too much zinc may cause adverse effects, including stomach pain and gut irritation.

It is also important to note that applying zinc to the skin has not been shown to be effective. This may be because zinc is not effectively absorbed through the skin.

SUMMARY

Individuals with acne tend to have lower zinc levels than people with clear skin. Several studies show that taking zinc orally can significantly reduce acne.

3. Make A Honey And Cinnamon Mask

Both honey and cinnamon are excellent sources of anti-oxidants.

Studies have found applying antioxidants to the skin is more effective at reducing acne than benzoyl peroxide and retinoids.

These are two common acne medications for the skin that have antibacterial properties.

The antioxidants studied were vitamin B3, linoleic (omega-6) fatty acid and sodium ascorbyl phosphate (SAP), which is a vitamin C derivative.

These specific antioxidants are not found in honey or cinnamon, but there is a possibility that other antioxidants may have a similar effect.

Honey and cinnamon also have the ability to fight bacteria and reduce inflammation, which are two factors that trigger acne.

While the anti-inflammatory, antioxidant and antibacterial properties of honey and cinnamon may benefit acne-prone skin, no studies exist on their ability to treat acne.

How to Make a Honey

and Cinnamon Mask

1. Mix 2 tablespoons honey and 1 teaspoon cinnamon together to form a paste.
2. After cleansing, apply the mask to your face and leave it on for 10–15 minutes.
3. Rinse the mask off completely and pat your face dry.

SUMMARY

Honey and cinnamon have anti-inflammatory, antioxidant and antibacterial properties. Because of this, they may be beneficial for acne-prone skin.

4. Spot Treat With Tea Tree Oil

Tea tree oil is an essential oil that is extracted from the leaves of Melaleuca alternifolia, a small tree native to Australia.

It is well known for its ability to fight bacteria and reduce skin inflammation.

What's more, several studies show that applying 5% tea tree oil to the skin effectively reduces acne.

When compared to 5% benzoyl peroxide, 5% tea tree oil did not act as quickly, but it did significantly improve acne after three months of use.

It also resulted in fewer adverse effects like dryness, irritation and burning, compared to benzoyl peroxide.

Tea tree oil is very potent, so always dilute it before applying it to your skin.

How to Use It

1. Mix 1 part tea tree oil with 9 parts water.
2. Dip a cotton swab into the mixture and apply it to affected areas.
3. Apply moisturizer if desired.
4. Repeat this process 1–2 times per day, as needed.

SUMMARY

Tea tree oil has strong anti-bacterial and anti-inflammatory properties. Applying it to the skin has been shown to reduce acne.

5. Apply Green Tea To Your Skin

Green tea is very high in antioxidants, and drinking it can promote good health.

There aren't any studies exploring the benefits of drinking green tea when it comes to acne, but applying it directly to the skin has been shown to help.

This is likely because the flavonoids and tannins in green tea are known to help fight bacteria and reduce inflammation, which are two main causes of acne.

The major antioxidant in green tea — epigallocatechin-3-gallate (EGCG) — has been shown to reduce sebum production, fight inflammation and inhibit the growth of P. acnes in individuals with acne-prone skin.

Multiple studies have shown that applying a 2–3% green tea extract to the skin significantly reduces sebum production and pimples in those with acne.

You can buy creams and lotions that contain green tea, but it is just as easy to make your own mixture at home.

How to Use It

1. Steep green tea in boiling water for 3–4 minutes.
2. Allow tea to cool.
3. Using a cotton ball, apply tea to skin or pour into a spray bottle to spritz on.
4. Allow to dry, then rinse with water and pat dry.

You can also add the remaining tea leaves to honey and make a mask.

Even though there isn't any evidence that drinking green tea can fight acne, some research suggests it may still be beneficial.

For example, drinking green tea has been shown to lower blood sugar and insulin levels, which are factors that can contribute to the development of acne.

SUMMARY

Green tea is high in antioxidants that help fight bacteria and reduce inflammation. Applying green tea to the skin has been shown to significantly reduce acne.

6. Apply Witch Hazel

Witch hazel is extracted from the bark and leaves of the North American witch hazel shrub, Hamamelis virginiana. It contains tannins, which have strong antibacterial and anti-inflammatory properties.

That's why it's used to treat a broad range of skin conditions, including dandruff, eczema, varicose veins, burns, bruises, insect bites and acne.

Unfortunately, there aren't any studies on the ability of witch hazel to treat acne specifically.

However, there are several studies that show applying witch hazel to the skin can fight bacteria, reduce inflammation and help with healing.

How to Use It

1. Combine 1 tablespoon witch hazel bark and 1 cup water in a small saucepan.
2. Soak witch hazel for 30 minutes and then bring the mixture to a boil on the stove.
3. Reduce to a simmer and cook, covered, for 10 minutes.
4. Remove the mixture from the heat and let sit for an additional 10 minutes.
5. Strain and store the liquid in a sealed container.
6. Apply to clean skin using a cotton ball 1–2 times per day, or as desired.

Nevertheless, it is important to note that commercially prepared versions may not contain tannins, as they are often lost in the distillation process.

SUMMARY

Applying witch hazel to the skin has been shown to fight bacteria, reduce inflammation and help heal the skin. It may be beneficial for individuals with acne, but more research is needed.

7. Moisturize With Aloe Vera

Aloe vera is a tropical plant whose leaves produce a clear gel.

The gel is often added to lotions, creams, ointments and soaps. It's commonly used to treat abrasions, rashes, burns and other skin conditions.

When applied to the skin, aloe vera gel can help heal wounds, treat burns and fight inflammation.

Aloe vera also contains salicylic acid and sulfur, which are both used extensively in the treatment of acne.

Several studies have shown that applying salicylic acid to the skin significantly reduces acne.

Similarly, applying sulfur has been proven to be an effective acne treatment.

While research shows great promise, the anti-acne benefits of aloe vera itself require further scientific evidence.

How to Use It

1. Scrape the gel from the aloe plant out with a spoon.
2. Apply gel directly to clean skin as a moisturizer.
3. Repeat 1–2 times per day, or as desired.

You can also buy aloe vera gel from the store, but make sure it is pure aloe without any added ingredients.

SUMMARY

When applied to the skin, aloe vera gel can help heal wounds, treat burns and fight inflammation. It may be beneficial for individuals with acne-prone skin, but more research needs to be done.

8. Take A Fish Oil Supplement

Omega-3 fatty acids are incredibly healthy fats that offer a multitude of health benefits.

You must get these fats from your diet, but research shows that most people who eat a standard Western diet don't get enough of them.

Fish oils contain two main types of omega-3 fatty acids: eicosapentaenoic acid (EPA) and docosahexaenoic acid (DHA).

EPA benefits the skin in several ways, including managing oil production, maintaining adequate hydration and preventing acne.

High levels of EPA and DHA have been shown to decrease inflammatory factors, which may reduce the risk of acne.

In one study, 45 individuals with acne were given omega-3 fatty acid supplements containing both EPA and DHA daily. After 10 weeks, acne decreased significantly.

There is no specific recommended daily intake of omega-3 fatty acids, but most health organizations recommend healthy adults consume a minimum of 250–500 mg of combined EPA and DHA daily.

You can also get omega-3 fatty acids by eating salmon, sardines, anchovies, walnuts, chia seeds and ground flaxseeds.

SUMMARY

Fish oils contain EPA and DHA omega-3 fatty acids. Taking a fish oil supplement may help decrease acne.

9. Exfoliate Regularly

Exfoliation is the process of removing the top layer of dead skin cells. It can be achieved mechanically by using a brush or scrub to physically remove the cells. Alternatively, it can be removed chemically by applying an acid that dissolves them.

Exfoliation is believed to improve acne by removing the skin cells that clog up pores.

It is also believed to make acne treatments for the skin more effective by allowing them to penetrate deeper, once the topmost layer of skin is removed.

Unfortunately, the research on exfoliation and its ability

to treat acne is limited.

Some studies show that microdermabrasion, which is a method of exfoliation, can improve the skin's appearance, including some cases of acne scarring.

In one small study, 25 patients with acne received eight microdermabrasion treatments at weekly intervals. Based on before and after photos, this helped improve acne.

96% of the participants were pleased with the results and would recommend the procedure to others. Yet while these results indicate that exfoliation may improve acne, more research is needed.

There are a wide variety of exfoliation products available in stores and online, but it's just as easy to make a scrub at home using sugar or salt.

How to Make a Scrub at Home

1. Mix equal parts sugar (or salt) and coconut oil.
2. Scrub skin with mixture and rinse well.
3. Exfoliate as often as desired up to once daily.

SUMMARY

Exfoliation is the process of removing the top layer of dead skin cells. It may reduce the appearance of scars and discolouration, but more research needs to be done on its ability to treat acne.

10. Follow A Low Glycaemic Load Diet

The relationship between diet and acne has been debated for years.

Recent evidence suggests that dietary factors, such as insulin and glycaemic index, may be associated with acne.

A food's glycaemic index (GI) is a measure of how quickly it raises blood sugar.

Eating high-GI foods causes a spike in insulin, which is thought to increase sebum production. Because of this, high-GI foods are believed to have a direct effect on the development and severity of acne.

Foods with a high glycaemic index include white bread, sugary soft drinks, cakes, doughnuts, pastries, candies, sugary breakfast cereals and other processed foods.

Foods with a low glycaemic index include fruits, vegetables, legumes, nuts and whole or minimally processed grains.

In one study, 43 people followed either a high- or low-glycaemic diet. After 12 weeks, the individuals consuming a low-glycaemic diet had a significant improvement in both acne and insulin sensitivity, compared to those eating carb-dense foods (62).

Another study with 31 participants yielded similar results.

These small studies suggest that a low-glycaemic diet may be helpful for individuals with acne-prone skin, but further research is needed.

SUMMARY

Eating high-glycaemic foods may increase sebum production and contribute to acne. More research is needed to determine whether a low-glycaemic diet can effectively treat or prevent acne.

11. Cut Back On Dairy

The Relationship Between Dairy And Acne Is Highly Controversial.

Drinking milk and consuming dairy products exposes you to hormones, which may cause hormonal changes and lead to acne.

Two large studies reported that higher levels of milk consumption were associated with acne.

However, participants self-reported the data in both of these studies, so more research needs to be done in order to establish a true causal relationship.

SUMMARY

Some studies found a positive association between drinking milk and acne. Limiting milk and dairy consumption may be a good idea for those with acne-prone skin, but more research needs to be done.

12. Reduce Stress

The hormones released during periods of stress may increase sebum production and skin inflammation, making acne worse.

In fact, multiple studies have linked stress to an increase in acne severity.

What's more, stress can slow wound healing by up to 40%, which may slow the repair of acne lesions.

Certain Relaxation And Stress-Reduction Treatments Have Been Shown To Improve Acne, But More Research Needs To Be Done.

Ways to Reduce Stress

- Get more sleep
- Engage in physical activity
- Practice yoga
- Meditate
- Take deep breaths

SUMMARY

Hormones that are released during times of stress can make acne worse. Reducing stress may help improve acne.

13. Exercise Regularly

Exercise promotes healthy blood circulation. The increase in blood flow helps nourish the skin cells, which may help prevent and heal acne.

Exercise also plays a role in hormone regulation.

Several studies have shown that exercise can decrease stress and anxiety, both of which are factors that can contribute to the development of acne.

It's recommended that healthy adults exercise for 30 minutes 3–5 times per week. This can include walking, hiking, running and lifting weights.

Summary

Exercise promotes healthy blood circulation, regulates hormones and helps reduce stress.

The Bottom Line

> *Acne is a common problem with a number of underlying causes. However, conventional treatments can cause dryness, redness and irritation. Fortunately, many natural remedies can also be effective. The home remedies listed in this article may not work for everyone, but they just might be worth a try.*

Nevertheless, you may want to consult a dermatologist if you have severe acne.

HEADACHE

1. Drink Water

Inadequate hydration may lead you to develop a headache.

In fact, studies have demonstrated that chronic dehydration is a common cause of tension headaches and migraines.

Thankfully, drinking water has been shown to relieve headache symptoms in most dehydrated individuals within 30 minutes to three hours.

What's more, being dehydrated can impair concentration and cause irritability, making your symptoms seem even worse.

To help avoid dehydration headaches, focus on drinking enough water throughout the day and eating water-rich foods.

2. Take Some Magnesium

Magnesium is an important mineral necessary for countless functions in the body, including blood sugar control and nerve transmission.

Interestingly, magnesium has also been shown to be a safe, effective remedy for headaches.

Evidence suggests that magnesium deficiency is more common in people who get frequent migraine headaches, compared to those who don't.

Studies have shown that treatment with 600 mg of oral magnesium citrate per day helped reduce both the frequency and severity of migraine headaches.

However, taking magnesium supplements can cause digestive side effects like diarrhoea in some people, so it's best to start with a smaller dose when treating headache symptoms.

3. Limit Alcohol

While having an alcoholic drink may not cause a headache in most people, studies have shown that alcohol can trigger migraines in about one-third of those who experience frequent headaches.

Alcohol has also been shown to cause tension and cluster headaches in many people.

It's a vasodilator, meaning it widens blood vessels and allows blood to flow more freely.

Vasodilation may cause headaches in some people. In fact, headaches are a common side effect of vasodilators like blood pressure medications.

Additionally, alcohol acts as a diuretic, causing the body to lose fluid and electrolytes through frequent urination. This fluid loss can lead to dehydration, which can cause or worsen headaches.

4. Get Adequate Sleep

Sleep deprivation can be detrimental to your health in many ways, and may even cause headaches in some people.

For example, one study compared headache frequency and severity in those who got less than six hours of sleep per night and those who slept longer. It found that those who got less sleep had more frequent and severe headaches.

However, getting too much sleep has also been shown to trigger headaches, making getting the right amount of rest important for those looking for natural headache prevention.

For maximum benefits, aim for the "sweet spot" of seven to nine hours of sleep per night.

5. Avoid Foods High In Histamine

Histamine is a chemical found naturally in the body that plays a role in the immune, digestive and nervous systems.

It's also found in certain foods like aged cheeses, fermented food, beer, wine, smoked fish and cured meats.

Studies suggest consuming histamine may cause migraines in those who are sensitive to it.

Some people are not able to excrete histamine properly because they have impaired function of the enzymes responsible for breaking it down.

Cutting histamine-rich foods from the diet may be a useful strategy for people who get frequent headaches.

6. Use Essential Oils

Essential oils are highly concentrated liquids that contain aromatic compounds from a variety of plants.

They have many therapeutic benefits and are most often used topically, though some can be ingested.

Peppermint and lavender essential oils are especially helpful when you have a headache.

Applying peppermint essential oil to the temples has been shown to reduce the symptoms of tension headaches.

Meanwhile, lavender oil is highly effective at reducing migraine pain and associated symptoms when applied to the upper lip and inhaled.

7. Try A B-Complex Vitamin

B vitamins are a group of water-soluble micronutrients that play many important roles in the body. For example, they contribute to neurotransmitter synthesis and help turn food into energy.

Some B vitamins may have a protective effect against headaches.

Several studies have shown that the B vitamin supplements riboflavin (B2), folate, B12 and pyridoxine (B6) may reduce headache symptoms.

B-complex vitamins contain all eight of the B vitamins and are a safe, cost-effective way to naturally treat headache symptoms.

B vitamins are considered safe to take on a regular basis, as they are water soluble and any excess will be flushed out through the urine.

8. Soothe Pain With A Cold Compress

Using a cold compress may help reduce your headache symptoms.

Applying cold or frozen compresses to the neck or head area decreases inflammation, slows nerve conduction and constricts blood vessels, all of which help reduce headache pain.

In one study in 28 women, applying a cold gel pack to the head significantly reduced migraine pain.

To make a cold compress, fill a waterproof bag with ice

and wrap it in a soft towel. Apply the compress to the back of the neck, head or temples for headache relief.

9. Consider Taking Coenzyme Q10

Coenzyme Q10 (CoQ10) is a substance produced naturally by the body that helps turn food into energy and functions as a powerful antioxidant.

Studies have shown that taking CoQ10 supplements may be an effective and natural way to treat headaches.

For example, one study in 80 people demonstrated that taking 100 mg of CoQ10 supplements per day reduced migraine frequency, severity and length.

Another study including 42 people who experienced frequent migraines found that three 100-mg doses of CoQ10 throughout the day helped decrease migraine frequency and migraine-related symptoms like nausea.

10. Try An Elimination Diet

Studies suggest that food intolerances can trigger headaches in some people.

To discover if a certain food is causing frequent headaches, try an elimination diet that removes the foods most related to your headache symptoms.

Aged cheese, alcohol, chocolate, citrus fruits and coffee are among the most commonly reported food triggers in people with migraines.

In one small study, a 12-week elimination diet decreased the number of migraine headaches people experienced. These effects started at the four-week mark.

11. Drink Caffeinated Tea Or Coffee

Sipping on beverages that contain caffeine, such as tea or coffee, may provide relief when you are experiencing a headache.

Caffeine improves mood, increases alertness and constricts blood vessels, all of which can have a positive effect on headache symptoms.

It also helps increase the effectiveness of common medications used to treat headaches, such as ibuprofen and acetaminophen.

However, caffeine withdrawal has also been shown to cause headaches if a person regularly consumes large amounts of caffeine and suddenly stops.

Therefore, people who get frequent headaches should be mindful of their caffeine intake.

12. Try Acupuncture

Acupuncture is a technique of Traditional Chinese medicine that involves inserting thin needles into the skin to stimulate specific points on the body.

This practice has been linked to a reduction in headache symptoms in many studies.

A review of 22 studies including more than 4,400 people found that acupuncture was as effective as common migraine medications.

Another study found that acupuncture was more effective and safer than topiramate, an anticonvulsant drug used to treat chronic migraines.

If you're looking for a natural way to treat chronic headaches, acupuncture may be a worthwhile choice.

13. Relax With Yoga

Practicing yoga is an excellent way to relieve stress, increase flexibility, decrease pain and improve your overall quality of life.

Taking up yoga may even help reduce the intensity and frequency of your headaches.

One study investigated the effects of yoga therapy on 60 people with chronic migraines. Headache frequency and intensity were reduced more in those receiving both yoga therapy and conventional care, compared to those receiving conventional care alone.

Another study found that people who practiced yoga for three months had a significant reduction in headache frequency, severity and associated symptoms, compared to those who did not practice yoga.

14. Avoid Strong Smells

Strong odours like those from perfumes and cleaning products can cause certain individuals to develop headaches.

A study that involved 400 people who experienced either migraine or tension headaches found that strong odours, especially perfumes, often triggered headaches.

This hypersensitivity to odours is called osmophilia and common in those with chronic migraines.

If you think you may be sensitive to smells, avoiding perfumes, cigarette smoke and strongly scented foods may help decrease your chance of getting a migraine.

15. Try An Herbal Remedy

Certain herbs including feverfew and butterbur may reduce headache symptoms.

Feverfew is a flowering plant that has anti-inflammatory properties.

Some studies suggest that taking feverfew supplements in doses of 50–150 mg per day may reduce headache frequency. However, other studies have failed to find a benefit.

Butterbur root comes from a perennial shrub native to Germany and, like feverfew, has anti-inflammatory effects.

Several studies have shown that taking butterbur extract in doses of 50–150 mg reduces headache symptoms in both adults and children.

Feverfew is generally considered safe if taken in recommended amounts. However, butterbur should be treated with caution, as un-purified forms can cause liver damage, and the effects of its long-term use are unknown.

16. Avoid Nitrates And Nitrites

Nitrates and nitrites are common food preservatives added to items like hot dogs, sausages and bacon to keep them fresh by preventing bacterial growth.

Foods containing them have been shown to trigger headaches in some people.

Nitrites may trigger headaches by causing the expansion of blood vessels.

In order to minimize your exposure to nitrites, limit the amount of processed meats in your diet and choose nitrate-free products whenever possible.

17. Sip Some Ginger Tea

Ginger root contains many beneficial compounds, including antioxidants and anti-inflammatory substances.

One study in 100 people with chronic migraines found that 250 mg of ginger powder was as effective as the conventional headache medication sumatriptan at reducing migraine pain.

What's more, ginger helps reduce nausea and vomiting, common symptoms associated with severe headaches.

You can take ginger powder in capsule form or make a powerful tea with fresh ginger root.

18. Get Some Exercise

One of the simplest ways to reduce headache frequency and severity is to engage in physical activity.

Another large study including more than 92,000 people showed that a low level of physical activity was clearly associated with an increased risk of headaches.

There are many ways to increase your activity level, but one of the easiest methods is to simply increase the number of steps you take throughout the day.

The Bottom Line

Many people are negatively impacted by frequent headaches, making it important to find natural and effective treatment options.

Yoga, supplements, essential oils and dietary modifications are all natural, safe and effective ways to reduce headache symptoms.

While traditional methods like medications are often necessary, there are many natural and effective ways to prevent and treat headaches if you're looking for a more holistic approach.

HEARTBURN

The effectiveness of the various home remedies on soothing heartburn differs from person to person. Home remedies to relieve heartburn, also called acid reflux, include:

Apple Cider Vinegar

"Apple cider vinegar works for some, but makes it worse for others," reports Rouzer.

Swallowing a small amount (about a teaspoon) of unprocessed apple cider vinegar mixed with water may reduce the acidity level in the stomach.

But there's no scientific evidence to back up those claims.

> *Bottom line: Apple cider vinegar is safe to try for acid reflux as long as you use a small amount and the cider vinegar's diluted.*

Probiotics

"I recommend probiotics for a variety of gastrointestinal issues – like diarrhoea, bloating and gas – but not usually for acid reflux," says Rouzer. She cautions that it's important to purchase probiotics from a trusted supplement manufacturer. You want to be sure you're getting a quality product.

Bottom line: Test out probiotics for heartburn relief as long as they're from a reputable company.

Chewing Gum

A small study found that chewing sugar-free gum for 30 minutes after lunch or dinner could reduce acid levels in the esophagus. But for some people, peppermint gum can worsen symptoms. (See information on peppermint, below.)

Bottom line: There's no harm in chewing gum after a meal to see if it soothes acid reflux. You may want to avoid peppermint or spearmint flavours if you can't tolerate them.

Aloe Vera Juice

The gel from aloe vera leaves is known for soothing a sunburn – but what about a heartburn? Some people take aloe vera internally to reduce stomach acid and calm irritation. However, there's no research to indicate that aloe vera helps heartburn.

Bottom line: Try aloe vera juice as long as you buy it from a so you can be confident, you're getting a pure and safe product.

Bananas

Bananas are a bland, low-acid fruit that people often find to be gentle on the digestive system. "The vitamins in bananas help stop gastrointestinal spasms, but it's not clear whether they can affect acid reflux," says Rouzer.

Bottom line: If nothing else, bananas are a great snack food for most people. Testing whether bananas help your heartburn symptoms couldn't hurt.

Peppermint

"Peppermint relaxes the stomach," says Rouzer. "You may feel better after taking it. However, peppermint can also increase acid reflux symptoms in some people – because it may loosen the muscle that keeps liquids from flowing back up into the esophagus."

Bottom line: Whether peppermint is useful depends on the individual. You can try sipping tea or tak-

ing a peppermint pill, but if this remedy instead increases your acid reflux, consider trying ginger. Ginger is calming and reduces inflammation in the stomach. Both peppermint and ginger can help with diarrhoea, bloating and gas, too.

With the popularity of essential oils, some consider using peppermint or ginger essential oil as an aid for digestion. Speak with your healthcare provider before taking essential oils internally or topically. Essential oils can interact with medications, each person's body reacts differently to these oils, and because the oils are not regulated, there can be inconsistencies in what is the actual product purchased.

Baking Soda

A little baking soda mixed with water can reduce your stomach's acidity level, says Rouzer. It works like an over-the-counter antacid, but unlike those fruity delights, a baking soda concoction doesn't taste as good.

Bottom line: If you've got baking soda in your pantry, try this home remedy when you're desperate for relief from acid reflux.

Lifestyle Changes Help Heartburn?

The best way to avoid heartburn discomfort is to prevent it. These lifestyle changes can make a big difference:

- Avoid trigger foods: Foods that promote heartburn include fried and fatty foods, caffeine, chocolate, spicy foods and carbonated beverages.
- Lose weight: Being overweight increases the likelihood that you'll experience heartburn.
- Avoid eating late at night: Try to eat three hours before going to bed. At a minimum, you should wait at least one hour after eating. (Read How to stop nighttime eating for tips.)
- Elevate the bed: Physically lift the head of your bed about six to eight inches so you're sleeping on an incline. If that's not possible, use a wedge pillow for lift.
- Avoid alcohol and tobacco: These substances increase the chances of heartburn attacks.
- Wear looser clothing: Tight clothing can put pressure on your digestive system.

When Should I See A Doctor?

If you experience the following symptoms, which may be signs of a serious condition, seek immediate care:

- Severe chest pain
- Change in stool colour
- Bloody vomit
- Unexpected weight loss
- Trouble swallowing

Is It Just Heartburn or GERD?

Frequent heartburn can be a major issue. If you experience heartburn two or more times a week, you may have gastroesophageal reflux disease (GERD).

In this chronic condition, frequent exposure to stomach acid irritates and damages the esophagus. Over time, that can lead to problems such as difficulty swallowing. An estimated 40 percent of Americans report symptoms of GERD – but the condition can significantly improve with lifestyle changes.

If you've tried home remedies and lifestyle adjustments and still have frequent heartburn, consult with your family doctor or a gastroenterologist. There are multiple treatments that can help, including medications and minimally invasive surgery for acid reflux.

URINARY TRACT INFECTION

1. Get Your Fill Of Water And Water-Based Foods

One of the first things to do when you have a urinary tract infection is drink plenty of water. That's because drinking water can help flush away the bacteria that's causing your infection, according to the National Institute of Diabetes and Digestive and Kidney Diseases (NIDDK). It puts you on the right track for recovery.

Most people can be assured they're getting the water they need by simply drinking water when thirsty, according to the health and medicine division of the National Academies of Sciences, Engineering, and Medicine. But to be safe, you may want to make sure you're drinking at least six to eight 8-ounce (oz) glasses of water each day. General recommendations have suggested that women get about 91 oz of water daily and men get about 125 oz each day, including water from food, as also noted in that group's report.

2. Load Up On Vitamin C For A Healthy

Urinary Tract

Getting plenty of foods high in vitamin C is import-ant because large amounts of vitamin C make urine more acidic. This inhibits the growth of bacteria in your urin-ary tract, according to Johns Hopkins Medicine's health library. (5) However, if you have an active UTI, you may want to avoid citrus or other acidic foods. These foods are known to irritate the bladder, which is the last thing you need when you're having pain urinating.

3. Soothe Uti Pain With Heat

Inflammation and irritation from UTIs cause burning, pressure, and pain around your pubic area, says Kandis Rivers, MD, a urologist in the Henry Ford Health Sys-tem in Wast Bloomfield, Michigan. Applying a heating pad can help soothe the area. (3) Keep the heat setting low, don't apply it directly to the skin, and limit your use to 15 minutes at a time to avoid burns.

4. Cut Bladder Irritants From Your Diet

When you have a UTI, caffeine, alcohol, spicy food, ni-cotine, carbonated drinks, and artificial sweeteners can irritate your bladder further, making it harder for your body to heal, according to the Cleveland Clinic. (6) Focus on healthy foods, such as high-fibre carbohydrates (including oatmeal or lentil soup), that are good for your digestive health, says Holly Lucille, ND, RN, a naturopathic doctor in private practice in West Hollywood, California, and the author of Creating and

Maintaining Balance: A Woman's Guide to Safe, Natural Hormone Health.

5. Go Ahead, Empty Your Bladder Again

Every time you empty your bladder — even if it's just a small amount — you rid it of some of the bacteria causing the infection. (3) Keep making those bathroom runs, advises Dr. Rivers.

6. Consider Herbal Remedies

You may find some relief from taking the herb uva ursi (bearberry leaf), which is sometimes used as an herbal remedy for lower urinary tract infections. (7) But Rivers cautions that it should be taken only for short periods of time — five days or less — as it could cause liver damage.

It's important to note that even though bearberry leaf may help some, there have been no large randomized controlled trials (the gold standard when it comes to proving the effectiveness of a drug or treatment in medicine) testing it as a remedy for UTIs. (7)

Some preliminary research, including as a study published in 2016 in the European Review for Medical and Pharmacological Sciences, also suggests that D-mannose supplements may help to prevent and treat UTIs. (8,9) Researchers think it might keep bacteria from attaching to the walls of the urinary tract. D-mannose is a simple sugar found naturally in fruits, including oranges, apples, and cranberries.

Always be sure to check with your doctor before an herbal supplement. Supplements, herbs, and other medication you might be taking can cause side effects or may interact with one another. The effects can sometimes be serious.

7. Change To Healthier Daily Habits

Lifestyle changes matter because they can help you recover from a UTI and might prevent another infection, according to the NIDDK. (3)

- Quit smoking.
- Wear loose cotton clothing and underwear.
- Wipe yourself clean from front to back.
- Choose only fragrance-free personal hygiene products.

8. Cut Back On Meat And Poultry

Some studies, such as one published in August 2018 in the journal mBio, have linked contaminated poultry and meat to E.coli bacteria strains that can cause UTIs. (10) These studies haven't proven that eating meat or poultry causes UTIs. In fact, some E.coli can live in the intestines without causing any problems. However, bacteria from the gut can enter the urinary tract and cause infection. This risk is greater in women than men, because women have shorter urethras than men, meaning the bacteria has less distance to travel to reach the bladder.

Cutting back on meat and focusing on fruits and veggies

may slightly cut your risk of UTIs. According to a study of Buddhists in Taiwan, published in January 2020 in Scientific Reports, compared with nonvegetarians, vegetarians had a 16 percent lower risk of UTI. (11)

A Note About Cranberry Juice and UTIs

Cranberry juice or cranberry extract in supplemental form has long been used as a home remedy for UTIs.

The thought is that "the proanthocyanidins in cranberries may help prevent bladder infections by keeping the bacteria from clinging to the bladder wall," says Sonya Angelone, MS, RDN, a nutrition consultant based in San Francisco, and spokesperson for the Academy of Nutrition and Dietetics.

Yet there's scientific controversy over how effective cranberry juice is at preventing UTIs due to conflicting conclusions in studies on the topic, according to an article published in May 2016 in Advances in Nutrition. Some studies have found it might work, while others have found no effect.

> *"Bottom line, there is some evidence it may help, and it doesn't hurt to try it," says Angelone. Just be sure to choose unsweetened cranberry juice (the sugar in sweetened cranberry juices can actually feed a bacterial infection). Mix this with sparkling water or plain yogurt, she recommends.*

Another low-calorie option — choose a cranberry pill

that contains d-mannose, she says.

Are Bananas Good for UTIs?

The American Urological Association calls bananas a bladder-friendly food. (13) That's because bananas aren't likely to irritate the bladder in most people. Other bladder-friendly fruits and veggies include: pears, green beans, winter squash, and potatoes. While eating bananas may help to lessen bladder irritation, eating bananas alone won't make a UTI go away.

Can Onions Help UTIs?

Onions, especially raw ones, may cause bladder irritation in some people. (6) If you have an active UTI, eating foods that further irritate the already inflamed tissues of the urinary tract could make UTI symptoms worse.

Can Drinking Apple Cider Vinegar Treat UTIs?

Studies, such as one published in January 2018 in Scientific Reports, have shown that apple cider vinegar has some antibacterial and antifungal properties, but there's no scientific or medical evidence that drinking apple cider vinegar cures UTIs. (14) Drinking large amounts of apple cider vinegar could lead to throat irritation and tooth decay.

SORE THROAT

Sore throat occurs as part of the body's immune response to viral or bacterial infections.

The natural immune response leads to inflammation and swelling of the mucous membranes in the throat.

However, several natural remedies may provide relief, including some that are supported by scientific evidence.

Here are 15 natural sore throat remedies.

1. Marshmallow Root

A person can choose from a variety of natural remedies to help soothe a sore throat.

People have used extracts from the marshmallow plant, Althaea officinalis, to treat sore throats and other conditions since ancient times.

Its root contains a gelatine-like substance called mucilage that coats and lubricates the throat when a person swallows it.

Researchers have tested lozenges containing marshmallow root in animals and found them to be effective and nontoxic, even at very high doses. It may also help soothe a dry cough.

Marshmallow root infusion

Here is a recipe for a cold marshmallow root infusion to soothe a painful throat:

Ingredients:

- 1 litre (l) of cold water
- 1 ounce, or 28 grams (g), of dried marshmallow root

Directions:

1. Fill a jar with the cold water.
2. Place the marshmallow root in cheesecloth and tie it up in a bundle.
3. Lower the bundle into the water until it is completely submerged.
4. Place the tied end of the bundle over the lip of the jar, place the lid on the jar, and screw it on.
5. Infuse overnight, or for at least 8 hours, then remove the bundle.
6. Pour the desired amount into a glass. Add an optional sweetener of choice.

When it is ready, take sips throughout the day to help reduce symptoms.

Choosing high quality dried marshmallow root from a

reliable source is important.

Bottom line: Marshmallow has a long history of use for treating sore throats. Its root contains a gelatinous substance, called mucilage, which coats and soothes the throat.

2. Sage And Echinacea

Sage is a popular herb in cooking, but it also has several medicinal uses.

Sage, also called Salvia officinalis, originated in the Mediterranean. Now, people grow it around the world.

Sage may help with many inflammatory conditions, and controlled studies suggest that it can help relieve throat pain.

In one study, a sage-echinacea spray was slightly more effective at reducing throat pain than a chlorhexidine lidocaine spray. Neither treatment caused any negative side effects.

Echinacea is another herb that people use in traditional medicine. It can fight bacteria, reduce inflammation, and help treat respiratory conditions.

Sage-echinacea throat spray

Follow this recipe to make sage-echinacea throat spray at home:

Ingredients:

- 1 teaspoon (tsp) of ground sage
- 1 tsp of ground echinacea
- 1/2 cup of water

Directions:

1. Boil the water.
2. Place the sage and echinacea in a small jar, then fill it with boiling water.
3. Let it steep for 30 minutes.
4. Pour the mixture through a strainer. Add 1/2 cup of hard liquor if desired.
5. Place the mixture in a small spray bottle and spray into the throat every 2 hours or as needed.

Bottom line: Research suggests that a sage-echinacea spray can help relieve a sore throat as effectively as antiseptic medication spray.

3. Apple Cider Vinegar

Apple cider vinegar is a natural health tonic. It has been a staple in folk medicine remedies for centuries. Its main active ingredient, acetic acid, helps fight bacteria.

The ancient Greek physician Hippocrates, known as the father of medicine, prescribed a combination of apple cider vinegar and honey, called oxymel, to treat flu symptoms, such as coughs and sore throats (9).

To help relieve throat pain, drink 1 cup of warm water mixed with 1 tablespoon (tbsp) of apple cider vinegar and 1 optional tbsp of honey.

The possible risks of apple cider vinegar include tooth decay and digestive problems. here.

People can find apple cider vinegar in supermarkets, health stores, and online.

Bottom line: Apple cider vinegar has antibacterial properties and, when a person mixes it in small amounts with warm water, could help relieve a sore throat.

4. Saltwater Gargle

Gargling with salt water is a well-known natural remedy to get rid of a sore throat.

The salt helps reduce swelling by pulling water out of the throat tissue. It may also help kill harmful microbes in the throat.

Combine 1 cup of warm water with 1 tsp of salt and stir to dissolve. Gargle with a mouthful of this mixture for 30 seconds once per hour.

Bottom line: Gargling hourly with warm salt water may help reduce swelling and ease throat discomfort.

5. Honey

Honey is a sweetener that people often combine with other natural ingredients to soothe a sore throat.

People use honey as a medicine because it has anti-inflammatory, antioxidant, and antimicrobial effects.

In addition to helping fight infection and providing pain relief, honey can also make certain remedies taste better.

Honey may be especially effective when a person combines it with warm water and apple cider vinegar or herbs. Some people choose to use raw honey or manuka honey.

However, children under the age of 1 should avoid honey. Their guts have not yet acquired healthy bacteria that can fight off some germs, such as botulism spores, that sometimes occur in honey.

Also, people who avoid sugar or follow a low carb diet may want to choose another remedy, since honey is a form of sugar. It contains 17.3 g of carbohydrates per tablespoon.

Bottom line: Honey can help relieve throat pain, particularly when a person combines it with vinegar or herbs in warm water. Never give honey to children under 1.

6. Licorice Root

The licorice plant, also called Glycyrrhiza glabra, is native to Europe and South Asia.

Best known for its sweet flavour, licorice also has uses in traditional medicine.

It has properties similar to aspirin that may help reduce sore throat pain. It also has antiviral, antibacterial, and anti-inflammatory effects.

However, there is no research into its ability to relieve illness-related sore throats.

That said, studies have reported that after surgery, licorice could significantly reduce throat pain due to breathing tube removal.

One study found that gargling with licorice water before surgery reduced the risk of getting a sore throat by 50%, compared with gargling with sugar water.

To make licorice tea, combine ground licorice root with hot water, let it steep for 5 minutes, then strain it prior to drinking.

> *Bottom line: Drinking or gargling licorice tea may help soothe a sore throat.*

7. Lemon water

Lemon water is a refreshing beverage that may also reduce the throat pain that occurs during a cold or flu.

Lemon contains vitamin C and other powerful antioxidants. These compounds fight inflammation and reduce oxidative stress, which are common markers of disease.

Lemon also increases the amount of saliva the body produces, which can help keep the mucous membranes moist.

Try combining lemon with warm water and a little honey or salt water to maximize its benefits.

Bottom line: Lemon water contains vitamin C and compounds that can soothe a sore throat and assist with healing.

8. Ginger Root Tea

Ginger is a spice with antibacterial and anti-inflammatory effects that may help relieve throat pain. Some, laboratory studies have found that ginger extract can kill some bacteria and viruses that cause respiratory illnesses. It can also reduce inflammation in people with tuberculosis, which is a lung disease.

Ginger tea is available from most markets and online retailers. People can also make their own from fresh ginger.

Ginger root tea

Follow this recipe to make ginger root tea at home:

Ingredients:

- fresh ginger root
- 1 l of water
- 1 tbsp (21 g) of honey or a sweetener of choice
- a squeeze of lemon juice

Directions:

1. Peel the ginger root and grate it into a small bowl.
2. Boil the water in a large saucepan, then remove it from the heat.
3. Place 1 tbsp of grated ginger into the saucepan and cover it with a lid.
4. Let it steep for 10 minutes.
5. Add the sweetener and lemon juice, then stir to combine.

This tea works well reheated as needed or served cold.

Bottom line: Ginger root tea may help fight infection, reduce inflammation, and relieve sore throat pain.

9. Coconut Oil

Coconut oil is a versatile food with several health benefits.

Animal studies suggest that it may help fight infection and reduce inflammation in areas exposed to it (19, 20).

Coconut oil is also very soothing because it helps lubricate the mucous membranes in the throat.

Here are a few ideas to try:

- Add a spoonful to hot tea or hot cocoa.
- Add a spoonful to soup.
- Put a spoonful in the mouth, allowing it to melt and coat the throat.

Limit coconut oil consumption to about 2 tbsp (30 millilitres [ml]) per day, as it can have a laxative effect at higher dosages. When using coconut oil for the first time, start with 1 tsp (5 ml) at a time to minimize potential side effects.

Bottom line: Coconut oil is very soothing on the throat and may have anti-inflammatory effects. Take up to 2 tbsp (30 ml) per day alone or in warm beverages.

10. Cinnamon

Cinnamon is a fragrant and delicious spice with a high antioxidant content. It can also provide antibacterial benefits.

In Chinese medicine, cinnamon is a traditional remedy for colds, flus, and sore throats.

Cinnamon tea is available for purchase in most grocery stores, in both herbal and regular varieties, and online . People can also add cinnamon to herbal or black tea.

Another option is to make cinnamon almond milk, which may be especially soothing for a sore throat.

Cinnamon almond milk

Follow this recipe to make cinnamon almond milk at home:

Ingredients:

- 1 cup of almond milk
- 1/2 tsp (2.5 ml) of ground cinnamon
- 1/8 tsp (0.6 ml) of baking soda
- 1 tbsp (15 ml) of honey or a sweetener of choice

Directions:

1. Place the cinnamon and baking soda in a saucepan and mix together.
2. Add the almond milk and mix again until it is well combined.
3. Heat the mixture until it just begins to simmer, then remove it from the heat.
4. Stir in the honey or sweetener.

Bottom line: Cinnamon may help fight throat pain

and infection due to a cold or flu. Try drinking cinnamon tea, or adding cinnamon to a warm beverage, to ease throat discomfort.

11. Plenty Of Fluids

Although swallowing may be uncomfortable, drinking plenty of water or other fluids will ultimately make the throat feel better. It is important to keep the throat's mucous membranes hydrated so that they can heal.

Drink tea, herbal infusions, water, or other beverages at whatever temperature feels most comfortable.

> *Bottom line: Staying hydrated, by drinking enough fluid through the day, will allow the throat to remain moist so that it can heal.*

12. Chicken Soup

Chicken soup is a well-known natural cold and sore throat remedy. It is also a comfort food that allows people to get more fluids when they are sick.

Try adding garlic to the soup. Garlic contains bioactive compounds that can also provide benefits during times of illness.

A person can buy canned chicken soup ahead of time and store it until needed, or they can prepare a homemade chicken soup.

Bottom line: Chicken soup is a comfort food that may help soothe a sore throat. Adding garlic may provide additional benefits.

13. Peppermint Tea

Peppermint tea contains anti-inflammatory compounds and is very soothing to the throat. The mint may also slightly numb the throat, thereby relieving pain.

Peppermint tea is caffeine-free, and its naturally sweet taste often requires no additional sweetener.

To make peppermint tea at home, steep fresh peppermint leaves in boiling water for 3–5 minutes, then strain off the leaves.

Bottom line: Peppermint tea is a tasty, refreshing beverage that may help reduce inflammation and throat discomfort.

14. Chamomile Tea

Chamomile is a daisy-like plant that people have used for medicinal purposes since ancient times.

Some research suggests that chamomile tea promotes restful sleep, which is important for healing.

Other studies have found that chamomile may help fight

infection and reduce pain.

Chamomile tea has a pleasant, mild aroma and flavour. Like other herbal teas, chamomile contains no caffeine.

Bottom line: Chamomile tea may promote restorative sleep, help fight infection, and soothe sore throat pain.

15. Herbal Lozenges

Teas, infusions, and other drinks are soothing and provide hydration, but sometimes sucking on a throat lozenge can also be comforting.

There are herbal throat lozenges available for purchase online and in some natural grocery stores. People can also make homemade throat lozenges with some of the herbs listed in this article.

Slippery elm is a popular herb for lozenges. It contains mucilage that coats and soothes the throat, similar to marshmallow root.

Try making lozenges ahead of time to have them on hand when a sore throat develops.

Bottom line: Purchase herbal throat lozenges or make a batch ahead of time to stay prepared for a sore throat.

Medications

Over-the-counter medications also can help ease a sore throat, including:

- Nonsteroidal anti-inflammatory drugs (NSAIDs): NSAIDs relieve inflammation and sore throat pain without causing stomach discomfort. Two common types are ibuprofen and aspirin.
- Sprays: Lidocaine sprays and other numbing throat sprays can effectively reduce throat pain.
- Lozenges: Throat lozenges containing lidocaine or other types of numbing medicine can help soothe a sore throat.

Bottom line: Several medications — including NSAIDs, throat sprays, and lozenges — can provide relief from a sore throat. These are available in stores and online.

Take-home message

No matter how healthy a person is, everyone gets a sore throat occasionally.

However, there are many steps a person can take to soothe a sore throat and encourage healing.

Be sure to see a doctor if a sore throat lasts for longer than a few days or is extremely painful. Severe or persistent pain may indicate strep throat, tonsillitis, or another serious infection that requires medical treatment.

ASTHMA

Home Remedies for Asthma are:

1)Make Changes To Your Diet

There is no specific diet for asthma patients but the exclusion and inclusion of a few elements in your diet can make a considerable change. Being overweight has been known to affect and trigger asthma symptoms. Include lots of fruits and vegetables in your diet. To reduce the inflammation around your airways, consider sources rich in Vitamin C, Vitamin E, and beta- carotene. Omega 3 found in salmons, mackerels are also known to help with inflammation. If any particular food seems to make your symptoms much worse, make a note and avoid consuming it.

2)Using The Papworth Method

The Papworth method has been used since 1960 to help people with asthma. It is a type of breathing and relaxation technique. It makes use of the nose and diaphragm to develop breathing patterns that will suit the asthma patient. These breathing patterns can then be used while engaging in activities that can possibly flare up your asthma. Papworth method is a way of controlling 'over-breathing' that is basically rapid and shallow breaths taken at the top of the chest.

3)Practicing Buteyko Breathing Technique

This is also a system of breathing exercises. Buteyko Breathing Technique focuses on breathing out through the nose and not the mouth. Breathing out through the mouth can dry up the mouth and the airways very fast resulting in more problems. Practicing and using BBT also makes you less prone to suffering from respiratory infections. Buteyko Breathing Technique can also be instrumental in decreasing your asthma symptoms with the help of slow and gentle breathing through the nose.

4)Using Honey

Honey can be used during the winters as a remedy for cold. It can be used to soothe a sore throat and prevent coughing. Coughing can worsen symptoms of asthma. You should be careful during winters as not to catch a cold. Mix honey with hot tea and drink it or just have a spoon of it every morning with 2 or 3 tulsi leaves.

5)Have Garlic

Do you love the smell of garlic in food? Good for you because not only does garlic enhance the smell and flavour of food, it also has certain medical qualities. Garlic has great anti-inflammatory properties. In the case of asthma, the surrounding areas of the airways become swollen. Garlic can help to reduce the inflammation thus, reducing the symptoms of asthma. Put garlic in your food or sauté it with some Nigella and enjoy it as it soothes your airways and helps to open them up.

6)Include Ginger In Your Diet

Just like garlic, ginger has anti-inflammatory qualities too. A study conducted in 2013 showed that ginger supplements were able to ease symptoms of asthma. Having some ginger daily can help you get some relief. Add ginger in your tea during winters. You can also add ginger while cooking your food and reap its benefits.

7)Yoga And Practising Mindfulness

The benefits of yoga are manifold. If you want to get relief from your asthma symptoms, make sure you do yoga every single day. Yoga incorporates breathing and stretching exercises. It will help to increase your flexibility and also boost your overall fitness. Some yoga poses that can help open your throat and chest are the bound angle pose, bow pose, bridge pose, camel pose, cat pose, cobra pose, cow pose, and cat pose among many others. Meditate every day and increase focus on your mind and body. The focus on breath and stress control from yoga and meditation will help you a lot in breathing easily.

8)Turmeric

Are you prone to many allergens? Developing various kinds of allergies can worsen your symptoms of asthma. Turmeric has been known to have strong anti-allergy properties. Histamines are known to cause inflammation. Turmeric has an effect on histamines that can stop inflammation. It can relieve symptoms of asthma and help you in preventing asthma attacks. Cook your food with turmeric every day.

9)Caffeine Intake

Caffeine has many similarities to theophylline. Theophylline is a bronchodilator drug that is used to open up the airways in the lungs of asthma patients. Because of its similarities to the drug, caffeine can be a good home remedy that can help you ease your asthma symptoms. Caffeine can be found in coffee, tea, cocoa, and various cola drinks. Hot beverages also help open up congested airways. Drink hot tea or coffee to feel and breathe better.

10)Take Steam Baths

Steam baths are often used to alleviate nasal and chest congestion. Steam treatments are not a treatment for asthma but can definitely improve your condition. Steam baths can provide moisture to your airways, relieve you of the congestion, help you get rid of accumulated mucus and let you breathe more freely.

What Happens During Asthma Attacks?

Asthma attacks may start out as minor but if not managed effectively, can turn dangerous. During an asthma attack, the airways become swollen and constricted more than usual. Breathing properly becomes quite tough. Some signs of an asthma attack are:

- Wheezing while breathing in and out
- Extremely rapid breathing
- Consistent coughing
- Difficulty in talking
- Sweaty and pale face
- Chest tightness and pain

What Can Trigger an Asthma Attack?

Do you live with somebody who suffers from asthma attacks often? Or do you fall prey to the attacks instead? It is important to know what can trigger an attack so that you can avoid them and lessen the chance of having an attack. Following are some common triggers:

- pet hair
- pollen
- pollution
- smoke from burning grass or wood
- acid reflux (stomach acid flows back to food pipe

and causes heartburn)
- certain fragrances
- tobacco smoke
- dust
- mould
- cockroaches
- sinus allergies and infections
- bad weather (thunderstorms, high humidity, bad air quality)

Emergency Asthma Treatment at Home in Case of an Attack

- Do not lie down
- Sit up straight and try to calm down
- Take a puff from a reliever every 30 to 60 seconds
- Breathe in through the nose and out through pursed lips (Pursed lip breathing)
- Breathe in through nose with hands placed on the belly and exhale (exhale should be longer than inhale)
- Try sipping warm back tea or coffee
- Try to inhale the vapor of eucalyptus essential oil from a diffuser
- Call for medical help

Try the natural home remedies for asthma and witness your symptoms get diminished. Write down about your symptoms when you experience them, foods that seem to trigger the symptoms, where you were and what you were doing before your asthma

*flared up, how often you have to use your inhaler, if
at all, and other such details..*

TYPHOID FEVER

1. Increase Fluid Intake

To prevent dehydration, keep sipping on fluids. Staying hydrated also helps in the timely elimination of waste materials and toxins from the body. Apart from water, have fruit juices, coconut water, and soups.

2. Use Cold Compresses

To combat high fever, use cold compresses to bring down the temperature. Sponge off armpits, feet, groin, and hands. Applying cold compresses on the extremities brings down the temperature most effectively.

3. Drink ORS

Ensure that you have WHO recommended ORS. Buy sachets from any chemist or keep deliciously flavoured tetra packs at home. You can even make at home by mixing sugar and salt in a liter of boiled water.

4. Have Apple Cider Vinegar

Apple cider vinegar helps to maintain a proper pH in the body. It draws out heat from the skin and therefore, reduces the body temperature. The loss of minerals because of diarrhoea is compensated by having apple cider vinegar. Mix a teaspoon in water. Add honey if needed. Drink before meals.

5. Basil

The holy basil is antibiotic and antimicrobial. Add basil to boiled water and drink three to four cups daily. Basil boosts immunity and calms the tummy. Or you can 4-5 basil/ tulsi leaves to make a paste. Add pepper powder to this paste and a few strands of saffron or Kesar. Mix all these and divide them into three parts. Have this mixture after every meal.

6. Garlic

Garlic speeds up recovery from typhoid due to its anti-oxidative properties. It boosts immunity and detoxifies the body. Eat two cloves on an empty stomach. This is not conducive for pregnant women and children.

7. Bananas

Bananas have pectin, a soluble fibre that helps the intestines absorb fluids, thus curing diarrhoea. Potassium in the fruit helps in replacing the electrolytes lost through loose motions. It is one of the best things to eat when having typhoid.

8. Triphala Churan

This is an essential ayurvedic churan that shows positive effects on fever and typhoid. It hampers the growth of Salmonella typhi. Chemists provide this in the form of powder and tablets.

9. Cloves

Cloves fight against bacteria that cause typhoid. Boil water with cloves, strain in a cup and have two cups daily.

10. Pomegranates

Pomegranates are an effective home remedy against typhoid. It helps in preventing dehydration. Have it as a fruit or take out the juice.

Consult a doctor and use the home remedies as an adjunct therapy. With proper rest, light food, clean water, and patience, the patient will recover quickly.

Tips to follow:

1. Avoid using items used by the infected person. E.g., towel, glass, napkin, etc.
2. Drink only boiled water.
3. Do not indulge in sweetened beverages and a big NO to coffee.

DANDRUFF

Let us first understand some common causes of Dandruff:

- Stress
- Illnesses such as eczema, Parkinson's disease
- Irregular and wrong methods of brushing
- Improper diet
- Irregular hair shampooing

Easy to implement home remedies to remove dandruff:

- ## Baking Soda

The noble and straightforward baking soda can act as an effective remedy to combat Dandruff. All you need to do is dampen your hair and sprinkle a handful of baking soda on your scalp. Rub vigorously. Post the exercise, go for a quick rinse, but avoid shampooing. Initially, after a few sessions, you feel your hair dry. But eventually, your scalp will start producing natural oils thereby making your hair look softer and devoid of dry flakes.

- ## Aspirin

The readily available Aspirin can play a significant role in keeping Dandruff at bay. Crush two Aspirins into a fine powder and add it to your regular shampoo. Shampoo your hair with this mixture and rinse after two to three minutes. The Salicylic Acid present in Aspirin helps to treat Dandruff efficiently.

• Yoghurt

A fresh bowl of yoghurt too can help in calming down an itchy scalp. All you need to do is shampoo your hair, apply the yoghurt, and let it rest for 15 minutes or so. Rinse with water and wash again with a small amount of your regular shampoo. Yoghurt is a treasure trove of friendly bacteria and thus helps to prevent flaking of the scalp area. You can also add black pepper to the yoghurt since it too has anti-fungal properties.

• Fuller's Earth

Fuller's Earth can absorb oil, grease, and dust. All these cause and increase the spreading of Dandruff. Simultaneously, Fuller's Earth also helps in improving blood circulation which helps to keep the scalp Dandruff-free. To make this mixture for your scalp, just mix a good proportion of Fuller's Earth with water and blend to make a smooth paste. Add a few drops of lemon juice to the paste. Apply this mixture to your scalp. Let it seep in for 20 minutes or so and then wash off with regular water.

• **Lemon**

This is by far the easiest of them all! Squeeze a full lemon and massage the juice into your scalp. Let it rest for 2 to 3 minutes and rinse off with a regular shampoo. You can also add lemon juice to a mug of water and use it as the last rinse post your hair wash session. Regularly repeat it till dandruff disappears. The acidic character of the Lemon helps to balance the pH of your hair.

• **Apple Cider Vinegar**

Apple Cider Vinegar is an effective natural remedy to get rid of dandruff. It is acidic in nature which helps to remove dead skin cells on the scalp. It also prevents the growth of fungus. Make a solution using 2 tablespoons of Apple Cider Vinegar in a cup of water. Wash your hair as usual with shampoo. Then pour this solution in your hair as the last rinse.

• **Aloe Vera**

Aloe Vera reduces skin irritation and has a moisturizing effect. It reduces flakiness and itchiness and gives relief from dandruff. It is antibacterial and antifungal which further protects from dandruff. Apply aloe vera gel directly on your scalp and leave for about half an hour. Later wash your hair with a mild shampoo.

• **Tea Tree Oil**

Tea Tree Oil reduces inflammation, itchiness and greasiness. It thus proves to be effective in decreasing dandruff. It is both antifungal and antimicrobial. Add around 5 to 10 drops of this oil to your regular bottle of shampoo and shake well. Rinse your hair well after shampooing.

• Organic Coconut Oil

Organic coconut oil is frequently used to prevent dandruff. It hydrates our scalp and prevents dryness and flakiness, which can increase dandruff. It is also antimicrobial and antifungal in nature. Gently massage organic coconut oil on
the scalp , leave for a few hours and then rinse using a mild shampoo.

• Neem

Antifungal, antimicrobial and anti-inflammatory properties of neem help to prevent and treat dandruff. Neem oil can be applied to the scalp and left for a few hours to prevent dandruff or you can make a hair mask out of neem. For the hair mask, grind neem leaves into a paste, leave this paste on the scalp for 15 to 20 minutes and then use a mild shampoo. You can also boil few neem leaves in water and use it to rinse your hair.

• Fenugreek Seeds

Fenugreek seeds are rich in protein, which prevent dryness, hair fall and dandruff. They also strengthen our hair roots and moisturize our scalp. Fenugreek seeds are key to long, thick and beautiful hair. Grind overnight soaked fenugreek seeds into a paste, apply on the scalp and hair, leave for 15 – 20 minutes and then clean using a mild shampoo.

FEVER

A fever is basically a symptom
of another condition or illness.
A fever can occur when your
body is fighting an infection,
such as the flu, or due to excess
accumulation of toxins.

Soaring temperatures, head ache, muscle ache, loss of appetite - a fever is never a pleasant experience for anybody. In addition to these common symptoms attached to fever, some people also suffer dehydration, weakness and slight shivering.

Whenever the body's temperature is higher than the normal range, the condition is called fever. For adults, 98.6 degrees Fahrenheit, or 37 degrees Celsius is generally considered normal, however, this may differ from body type to body type.

Some people tend to be on the higher end in terms of temperature. But generally, anybody having above 99 degrees Fahrenheit is said to have fever. A fever is basically a symptom of another condition or illness.

A fever can occur when your body is fighting an infection, such as the flu, or due to excess accumulation of toxins.

Ayurvedic expert Dr. Ashutosh Gautam says, "Few traditional herbs that Ayurveda recommends to treat fever are sudarshan leaves, ginger, giloy, tulsi (holy basil), neem, black pepper and cloves. Consumption of these have proven fruitful in relieving fever."

If the fever is on the higher end, and stays for more than three days, chances are that it could be due to a viral infection, chikunginya, dengue or malaria. In such cases it is better to consult with a doctor immediately.

However, in cases of mild fever, these home remedies may come handy:

1.Basil

Basil is an effective herb for bringing down fever. This herb is just as effective as many types of antibiotics in the market. Its healing properties will help reduce fever very quickly. Take about 20 basil leaves and boil them, now add 1 teaspoon of crushed ginger in the strained tulsi water, and boil until the solution gets reduced to half. Add a little honey and drink this tea two or three times a day for three days to get relief.

Basil is an effective herb for bringing down fever

2.Garlic

Garlic is packed with many antibacterial properties, according to the book Healing Foods by DK Publishing. "The main beneficial ingredients of this member of allium family are allicin and diallyl sulfides-sulfurous compounds that are antibacterial and antifungal". The warm nature of garlic can also lower high fever by promoting sweating. Crush 1 garlic clove and add it to 1 cup of hot water. Let it rest for 10 minutes, and then strain. Drink this twice a day for best results. Garlic is packed with many antibacterial properties

3.Ginger

The perennial herb native to China and India known as Zingiber officinale can prove to be an aid to a plenty of your health woes like cold, flu, inflammation, sore throat and fever. Its natural antiviral and antibacterial elements help fight the infection in your body and bolster your immunity from within. You can have it in a form of tea, by adding 1 1/2 teaspoon of grated ginger to 1 cup of boiling water. Add, some honey to flavour it, and drink this tea at least three or four times a day. Or, you can also mix together 1 1/2 teaspoon of ginger juice, 1 teaspoon of lemon juice and 1 tablespoon of honey. Have this concoction two to three times a day for best results. Its natural antiviral and antibacterial elements help bring down fever

4.Cilantro Leaves

According to The Complete Book of Ayurvedic Home Remedies by Dr. Vasant Lad, putting a handful of cilantro leaves in a blender with about 1/3rd cup of water, blended thoroughly and strained, can help alleviate symptoms of fever. Take 2 teaspoons of remaining liquid three times a day to help lower fever, instructs the book.

5.Grapes

"Grapes are cooling. Into 1 cup of grape juice, add 1/2 teaspoon cumin, 1/2 teaspoon fennel and 1/2 teaspoon sandalwood powder, and drink. This will help relieve fever," writes Dr. Vasant Lad in his book.Grapes are cooling, hence good remedy for fever.

6.Apple Cider Vinegar (Acv)

Apple cider vinegar is also said to work as an effective remedy for fever. The slightly acidic nature of the vinegar helps draw heat, leaving a cooling effect. The vitamins and minerals present in the ACV further helps replenish the body with minerals, which often gives way to the toxins. Mix 2 teaspoons of apple cider vinegar and 1 tablespoon of honey in a glass of water and drink the concoction at least two to three times a day for best results.

Remember, if these home remedies also do not work and your temperatures continue to soar, it is better to consult a doctor or a physician at the earliest.

KNEE PAIN

Knee pain is a common condition that can be caused by both short-term and long-term problems.

Many short-term knee problems do not need any help from doctors and people can often help with their own recovery.

Home remedies can also help with many of the long-term problems with knee pain.

Fourteen home remedies

The treatment for knee pain will depend, to some extent, on the cause of the problem.

However, the following simple remedies can help with many forms of knee pain.

1. Physical Activity

Exercises to strengthen the upper thighs can benefit the

knee joint.

Exercise can delay the development of osteoarthritis (OA), one of the most common causes of knee pain.

Walking, cycling, swimming, tai chi, and yoga may all be beneficial.

Being physically active boosts the health of cartilage tissue, whether a person has OA or not.

Exercise also strengthens the way the body supports the joints. Strengthening the leg muscles is especially beneficial for the knees.

People with joint pain can benefit from activities such as water aerobics, as this puts little strain on the knees.

2. Strengthening Exercises

Individuals can work with a physical therapist to identify the best exercises and programs for their needs.

Strengthening the upper leg muscles—the quadriceps muscles—through exercise can help to protect the knee joint. These muscles are at the sides and front of the thighs.

Here are some ways to strengthen these muscles:

- Straighten and raise a leg while lying or sitting down.
- Place one foot up on a step, then the other, stepping down again, and repeating the step-ups.

- Sit on a chair and then stand and sit repeatedly for a minute. Do this in a slow, controlled way and avoid using the hands to support you.
- Hold a chair and squat until the kneecaps cover the toes. Do this 10 times.

3. Posture And Support

Measures that can help to minimize knee strain include:

- avoiding low chairs and couches that you "sink" into
- sitting on a pillow to raise your seating level, if necessary
- checking that you have a good sitting posture, without slouching or leaning
- wearing supportive shoes and avoiding those with broken arches, as they can result in abnormal force and wear on the knee
- avoiding prolonged sitting and long periods without moving, as joints may become stiff and painful without movement

4. Weight Loss And Diet

A Mediterranean diet can help people maintain a healthy weight and may have anti-inflammatory properties.

People who have excess weight or obesity have a higher risk of knee pain.

Carrying extra weight gives the joints more work to do.

Losing it helps to reduce long-term knee pain, including pain caused by arthritis.

Extra weight on your body increases inflammation throughout the body and the knees are affected.

Eating well helps with keeping weight off.

A healthful diet means a balanced one that is:

- high in fruit, vegetables, and fibre
- low in meat, animal fat, and other fat

The Arthritis Foundation recommend a Mediterranean-style diet that is rich in fresh produce.

Experts urge people with OA of the knee to lose weight if they have overweight or obesity.

A doctor or dietitian can help decide how much weight a person needs to lose. They can also help plan a suitable diet.

5. Medications

Non-steroidal anti-inflammatory and other medications can help with knee pain caused by arthritis. Some of these need to be given in a doctor's office, but some can be used at home, either with or without a prescription.

Medications that may help manage pain include:

- oral or topical non-steroidal anti-inflammatory drugs (NSAIDs)
- topical capsaicin

- steroid injections into the joint
- tramadol

Acetaminophen and duloxetine, which is an antidepressant, may help.

Experts do not recommend using opioids, except for tramadol.

6. Massage

Massage, including self-massage, may relieve knee pain.

These should be done in a seated position with the knees pointing forward and the feet flat on the floor.

1. Loosely closing the hands into fists, tap the upper, lower, and middle thigh 10 times with both hands. Repeat three times.

2. Sitting with the feet flat on the floor, place the heel of the hand on the top of the thigh and glide it as far as the knee, then release. Repeat five times. Do the same for the outer and inner sides of the thigh.

3. Press four fingers into the knee tissue and move up and down five times. Repeat all around the knee.

4. Place the palm of the hand on top of the thigh, glide it down the thigh, over the knee and back up the outer thigh.

Massaging the thigh muscles will have a beneficial impact on the knee.

Current guidelines do not recommend massage as a treatment for OA of the knee, as there is not enough evidence to prove that it helps reduce symptoms. However, massage may offer other benefits, such as managing stress.

7. Aromatherapy Preparations

Essential oils may help reduce pain. A study published in 2008 suggested that massaging with an oil containing ginger and orange improved pain and function in knees with moderate to severe pain due to osteoarthritis. In one investigation, researchers found that applying an ointment containing cinnamon, ginger, mastic, and sesame oil had a similar effect on pain, stiffness, and motion as using salicylate ointment.

A range of essential oils is available for purchase online, including cinnamon, orange and ginger essential oil.

8. Protection, Rest, Ice, Compression, And Elevation (Price)

Use compression to support the knee and relieve pain.

Rest, ice, compression, and elevation may help treat mild knee pain that results from a soft tissue injury, such as a sprain.

Protection refers to protecting the knee from further injury, for example, by taking a break from the activity that caused it.

Rest can reduce the risk of further injury and give tissues time to heal. However, stopping all movement is not advisable, as this can lead to stiffness and, in time, muscle weakness.

Ice can help reduce swelling and inflammation. It should be wrapped in a cloth and applied for 20 minutes several times on the first day of injury. Never put ice directly the skin, as this can lead to further damage.

Compression with a knee support, for example, can increase comfort levels. The support or bandage should be firm but not tight.

Elevation, or keeping the leg raised, will encourage circulation and reduce swelling. Ideally, the knee should be above the level of the heart.

9. Heat And Cold

Heat and cold can be effective in treating pain in the lower back, and it has been recommended to ease joint pain that results from arthritis.

- Heat relaxes muscles and improves lubrication, leading to a reduction in stiffness. Use a hot water bottle or a warm pad.
- Ice, wrapped in a cloth, can reduce pain, inflammation, and swelling.

Some people may use heat to improve mobility in the morning and reduce swelling later in the day.

Remember to test any hot item before applying it, especially if it is for an older person or someone who cannot communicate easily.

10. Climate

A colder climate is often thought to worsen pain.

Study findings do not support this, although living in a pleasant climate might make pain psychologically easier. It may also provide easier opportunities to achieve a healthier lifestyle.

In 2014, researchers found that — rather than weather itself — sensitivity to weather in older people with osteoarthritis may affect how they experience joint pain.

People from Southern Europe, women, and those with higher anxiety levels were more likely to report weather sensitivity, and those with higher levels of sensitivity were more likely to report increased pain, especially with damp or rainy and cold weather.

The results of the study did not support the common belief that pain becomes worse in a colder climate.

A 2017 study carried out in the United States supported this view. Findings showed no link between rainfall and increased medical visits for joint pain.

11. Acupuncture

In 2017, a study involving 570 people found evidence

that acupuncture might help people with osteoarthritis in the knee.

Participants received either 23 true or 23 sham acupuncture sessions over 26 weeks, or 6 acupuncture sessions over 12 weeks.

Those who had true acupuncture scored higher in pain and function scores, compared with the others.

Researchers concluded:

"Acupuncture seems to provide improvement in function and pain relief as an adjunctive therapy for osteoarthritis of the knee when compared with credible sham acupuncture and education control groups."

The ACR and AF note that acupuncture may help ease pain.

12. Tai Chi

Tai chi is a form of meditative exercise, and the benefits of exercise alone are discussed above.

A year-long study of 204 participants with knee osteoarthritis concluded that tai chi might have similar, if not greater, benefits compared with standard physical therapy. The average age of participants was 60 years.

Improvements in primary outcome scores were recorded in both groups at 12 weeks, and these continued throughout the program.

In addition, those who did tai chi also saw significant improvements in symptoms of depression and the physical aspects of quality of life, compared with those who underwent standard physical therapy.

The ACR and AF strongly recommend tai chi as a form of exercise for people with OA of the knee.

13. Medical Marijuana

Recent approval of the use of cannabidiol (CBD), also known as medical marijuana, has provoked interest in it as a solution to a range of health problems.

CBD is not the compound in marijuana that produces psychotropic effects, but it does appear to have a number of pharmacological effects.

Animal studies have suggested that it may improve joint pain, because it:

- inhibits pain pathway signalling
- has anti-inflammatory effects

Clinical trials have not proven its safety or effectiveness for use in rheumatic disease, but researchers suggest it should not be ruled out as an option in the future.

14. Apple Cider Vinegar And Other Foods

According to some sources, apple cider vinegar (ACV) has anti-inflammatory properties that can help relieve arthritis and other types of pain.

However, there is a lack of scientific evidence to support this. The Arthritis Foundation refers to ACV as a "food myth."

Other popular advice for arthritis includes:

- consuming collagen, gelatine, or pectin, and raw foods.
- avoiding dairy, acidic foods, and nightshade vegetables, such as tomatoes, potatoes, and egg-plant

There is no evidence to suggest that these are helpful or even advisable.

Pain at the front of the knee

Pain at the front of the knee is one of the most common aches and pains. It is second only to lower back pain – around a quarter of people will get it at some point in their lives.

It commonly affects teenagers, especially young female athletes. It is the most common overuse syndrome in sportspeople.

Most cases of front knee pain are injuries from overuse, or from poor preparation for exercise. The problems usually go away on their own, and sporting activities can resume after the pain subsides.

The pain varies but tends to:

- be a dull ache that starts gradually, and is linked to activities
- produce clicking or other sounds
- come on when going upstairs, or when getting up after a long time sitting, squatting down, or kneeling
- produce a weakness in the legs

Recommended treatments for front knee pain include:

- stopping the activities that trigger it until it is resolved
- applying ice when the knee is painful
- taking over-the-counter pain relievers such as ibuprofen or naproxen
- using strengthening exercises

Causes of knee pain

Osteoarthritis, rheumatoid arthritis, sprains, and gout are some of the most common causes of knee pain.

Osteoarthritis

Osteoarthritis is one of the most common causes of long-term knee pain.

One common reason for long-term knee pain is a type of arthritis known as osteoarthritis. It is thought to be caused by wear and tear in the joint. It affects mostly older people over 65 years.

The knee bends and straightens smoothly because of the cartilage that covers the ends of the bones in the healthy joint.

Long-term damage to this cartilage leads to osteoarthritis. Movement becomes restricted and pain gradually increases.

The pain worsens on weight-bearing and is relieved with rest.

Pain also comes on after waking up or following periods without moving.

Movement reduces stiffness.

Rheumatoid Arthritis

Another kind of arthritis, rheumatoid arthritis (RA), can cause knee pain, too.

Rheumatoid arthritis tends to involve swelling of the knee. Sore joints will tend to be red, tender, warm, and swollen.

The pain involves more general stiffness that is typically worse in the early morning. There can be afternoon fatigue. Knee pain with these symptoms needs the attention of a doctor for correct diagnosis and treatment. Rheumatoid arthritis benefits from early treatment.

Sprains, Strains, And Injuries

Sprains and strains happen when tissues in the knee become stretched by unusual or increased activity, or an awkward twist or trip.

PRICE, described above, should lead to a reduction in pain and improved movement within days, and a gradual improvement over the weeks to follow.

A sprain often resolves itself, but some problems can require more treatment. For example, an injury to the pad of tissue in the knee joint known as the meniscus may require surgery.

Gout

Gout is another type of arthritis. It produces sudden episodes of severe knee pain with redness and swelling, and can affect other joints. The condition can be treated under medical care with medication and changes to diet and exercise.

When to see a doctor

An obvious knee injury caused by sudden trauma, such as from a road accident or a fall, may need immediate medical attention.

A knee should be checked by a doctor if there is considerable pain, deep cuts, swelling, or the person is unable to use their leg.

For other cases of knee pain, a doctor will need to examine the problem if it:

- persists for a long time
- gets progressively worse
- disrupts daily activities

It is important to get a diagnosis and treatment from a doctor if knee pain involves red, tender, warm, and swollen joints.

If the symptoms are persistent, involve other joints, and there are other symptoms such as morning stiffness, it could be rheumatoid arthritis. Doctors can give drugs for both the disease itself and the pain it causes.

If a swollen knee is very hot and painful, and if there are other general symptoms of feeling unwell, this is a time to get urgent medical help. The knee could be infected, and serious infection can be dangerous. This needs urgent hospital treatment.

Anyone whose knee pain is receiving medical help should see contact their doctor again if problems get worse or if there are issues with treatment, such as a drug side effect.

BRONCHITIS

Bronchitis is a common respiratory disease caused by viruses, bacteria, irritants such as smoke, and other particles that aggravate the bronchial tubes. These tubes bring air from the nose and mouth to the lungs.
You may be able to treat acute bronchitis on your own without medical treatment. In many causes, symptoms improve within two weeks.

It's important to treat your symptoms at the first sign of them to ensure a rapid recovery. With proper self-care, you should be able to bounce back quickly. But if the bronchitis worsens and your lungs sound congested, seek medical advice.

Home remedies

It's possible to treat acute bronchitis at home using natural remedies. Many of these methods may provide additional health benefits as well.

1. Ginger

Some researchers have found evidence that ginger can have an anti-inflammatory effect against respiratory infection. You can take ginger in several ways:

- Chew dried, crystallized ginger.
- Use fresh ginger to make tea.
- Eat it raw or add it to food.
- Take it in capsule form as directed.

It's safest to use ginger in a natural form, rather than in capsules or supplements. You may be sensitive to ginger, so take it in small amounts if you're not used to it. Eating occasional ginger is safe for everyone, but do not take ginger as a supplement or medication if you:

- are pregnant or breastfeeding
- have diabetes
- have heart problems
- have any type of blood disorder

: What are the benefits and side effects of ginger water?

2. Garlic

Garlic is said to have countless healing properties. Results of a 2016 study show that garlic effectively inhibited the growth of infectious bronchitis virus. This finding suggests garlic can be used as a natural remedy for bronchitis.

Fresh garlic is best, but if you dislike the taste you may take garlic in capsule form.

Use garlic with caution if you have a bleeding disorder. Always take it in small amounts to make sure it doesn't upset your stomach.

3. Turmeric

Turmeric is a spice often used in East Indian foods. A 2011 study found turmeric provided more anti-inflammatory effects than ginger. Turmeric also increases antioxidant activity. That means it may help reduce irritation and boost your immunity.

To take turmeric:

- Add fresh turmeric to salads or use it to make pickles.
- Mix 1/2 teaspoon of powdered turmeric with 1 teaspoon of honey to make a paste. Consume the paste 1 to 3 times per day while symptoms last.
- Take turmeric in capsule form as directed.
- Use powdered or fresh turmeric to make tea.

Using turmeric as a spice in food is usually safe unless you are sensitive. Do not use turmeric as a medication if you have:

- stomach issues
- gallbladder issues
- bleeding or blood disorders
- hormone-sensitive conditions
- iron deficiency

If you're pregnant or nursing, don't take turmeric in large amounts.

4. Steam

Steam helps break up mucus so you can expel it more easily. The easiest way to use steam is in the bath or shower. Make your shower as hot as you can handle, step in, then breathe deeply through your mouth and nose.

The hot water will also help relax muscles that may be tense from coughing. You can also visit a steam room at a gym or spa, if one's available and you have enough energy. It's best not to soak in a hot bath if you feel ill or short of breath.

Another steam option involves putting hot water in a bowl, covering your head with a towel, and inhaling the steam. Some people add a mentholated vapor rub to the hot water to help with moving mucus. The bowl-and-towel method can be dangerous, though, because the water could be hotter than you intended, which could cause the steam to burn your airways. Do not stay over the hot water for more than a minute or two at a time, and don't continue to heat the water.

5. Salt Water

Gargling salt water may help break up mucus and reduce pain in your throat. Dissolve a teaspoon of salt into a glass of warm water. Sip small amounts of the salt water and gargle at the back of your throat. Do not swallow the water. Instead, spit it out in the sink. Repeat as often as you like. Afterwards, you may want to rinse your mouth with plain water.

6. Sleep

Get plenty of sleep and allow your body to rest. It may be difficult to sleep soundly while fighting a cough, but take care to avoid any unnecessary activity. It is during the deep stages of sleep that you repair and enhance immune function so your body can better fight the inflammation.

7. Lifestyle Changes

A healthy lifestyle goes hand in hand with the prevention of illnesses. It can help you recover faster when you're sick, too. A minor illness may even be your body's way of telling you to slow down and take it easy.

The following changes may help improve your recovery and reduce your risk of getting sick in the future:

- Avoid smoking and second-hand smoke environments.
- Avoid polluted environments.
- Wear a surgical mask if you're exposed to pollution.
- Boost your immunity with a healthy diet.
- Exercise at least 3 times per week for a minimum of 20 minutes each time.
- Wash your hands frequently to prevent the spread of infection.
- Use a humidifier and clean it regularly following the manufacturer's guidelines.

Traditional treatments

You can pair over-the-counter (OTC) medications with the suggested natural remedies. The following medications may be helpful:

- aspirin (do not take aspirin if you take other blood thinner medications)
- ibuprofen (Advil, Motrin)
- acetaminophen (Tylenol)
- expectorant cough syrup

Antibiotics will only work if the bronchitis is caused by a bacterial infection. Antibiotics are not effective against viruses or irritant inflammation, so they're not usually used to treat bronchitis.

Symptoms of bronchitis

Bronchitis causes excess mucus production and a tightening of your airways. The increased phlegm can make it difficult to breath and cause a persistent cough.

The cough may be accompanied by the following symptoms:

- white or coloured mucus
- tightness in the chest
- shortness of breath
- fever
- chills
- muscle aches
- nasal congestion

- tiredness

Bronchitis often comes as you are healing from a cold or viral infection.

Chronic bronchitis

Long-term bronchitis occurs as a result of breathing environmental irritants. The number one cause is smoking. You may also develop chronic bronchitis from inhaling second-hand smoke or polluted air.

Long-term bronchitis could also result from an extended illness. Infants and older adults are especially prone to chronic bronchitis.

Chronic bronchitis occurs frequently and lasts at least 3 months out of a year for at least 2 years. It involves a wet cough for most days in a month.

If you have chronic bronchitis, you'll need medical care from a doctor or respiratory therapist. They'll help you work out a plan for managing your condition. It's important to treat chronic bronchitis because it leaves you vulnerable to other health complications.

When to see a doctor

If you think you aren't recovering at a normal rate, visit your doctor.

You may also consider seeing your doctor if you have:

- coughing that lasts more than a month
- extremely painful cough

- high fever
- difficulty breathing
- severe headache
- blood with your cough
- frequent cases of bronchitis

Outlook

Symptoms of acute bronchitis usually resolve within 1 to 2 weeks with home treatment.

You should start to feel noticeably better after a few days. A dry cough may last up to a month. Remember:

- Drink plenty of water and warm liquids, and eat healthy foods.
- Rest as much as possible until you feel completely healthy.
- Incorporate as many aspects of a healthy lifestyle into your daily routine to maintain your health.

If your symptoms do not improve with home care, or if you frequently develop bronchitis, see your doctor. You may need more aggressive treatment, or you may have chronic bronchitis.

HEART DISEASE

Now that we have a brief understanding of how heart disease can cause trouble, let us take a look at some of the common herbal remedies for heart disease prevention.

Moving on to some interesting heart disease prevention tips....

1. Green Tea:

Time and again, Green tea has emerged as one of the most powerful natural remedies for numerous ailments. It is well recognised for its high antioxidant content which has the capability of fighting harmful free radicals that are responsible for heart disease.

The chief antioxidant that is present in green tea is epigallocatechin gallate (EGCG). It has the capability of combating harmful toxins that are generated in the body from numerous physiological processes and digestion of foods. Not only that, harmful toxins called free radicals are generated on exposure to environmental factors such as pollution and smog.

Clinical studies suggest that drinking 5 to 6 cups of green tea per day is essential to reap the benefits of its heart protection capabilities.

2. Turmeric:

Turmeric is a natural spice that is abundantly present in Indian cooking. Turmeric contains the active ingredient curcumin which has powerful properties that can protect the heart muscle. Curcumin is responsible for the yellow colour of turmeric.

The benefits of a regular turmeric consumption as a part of your daily diet is not just limited to heart protection. Curcumin has demonstrated in numerous studies to have anti-inflammatory, anti-cancer and antioxidant properties. Not just that, it has an effect on thinning the blood through its antithrombotic properties.

A recent study has found that it may even improve your memory power and delay memory loss and Alzheimer's disease.

A large part of heart attacks and heart disease is the narrowing of blood vessels i.e. atherosclerosis. As I have previously mentioned in this article, atherosclerosis is a result of underlying inflammation.

Curcumin in turmeric has anti-inflammatory properties that can in a sense reduce inflammation and atherosclerosis. This means that by regularly consuming turmeric as a part of your diet, you could protect your heart from heart disease.

It is simple to have your daily dose of turmeric. You

could sprinkle the required amount in your curry or even add a small teaspoon of it to a glass of milk prior to consumption.

Clinical studies have also shown that regular use of curcumin in turmeric can inhibit certain pathways that are responsible for thickening and weakening of the heart muscle. Not just that, curcumin may also prevent the development of irregular heart rhythms by correcting the quantity of calcium that enters the heart muscle.

The use of curcumin can be particularly helpful in individuals who are obese or who suffer from a condition called metabolic syndrome. Metabolic syndrome consists of a combination of high blood pressure, diabetes, obesity, high cholesterol and a spectrum of other problems that are all risk factors in heart attacks.

By exerting anti-inflammatory effects, curcumin can protect your heart from prematurely ageing. In one particular study, it is found that curcumin could reduce triglycerides which is a type of fat responsible for coronary artery disease. Not just that, it can also increase the levels of good cholesterol i.e. HDL cholesterol. Lower energy cholesterol i.e. bad cholesterol levels were also seen.

Finally, curcumin can also reduce the risk of developing heart failure. In heart failure, the heart muscle becomes enlarged and is unable to function efficiently as a pump. This is particularly relevant in individuals who suffer from type II diabetes. The high blood sugars in diabetes can damage the heart muscle by exerting oxidative stress. This can be prevented by curcumin in turmeric.

In short, turmeric has numerous health benefits and can in particular protect the heart.

3. Garlic:

Garlic (Allium sativum) has achieved a formidable status in the world of medicinal history as an agent that has a number of therapeutic benefits. In fact, the history of garlic dates back to the Egyptian times where it was used to treat conditions such as worms, tumours and even heart disorders.

Garlic is rich not just in carbohydrates but also contains moderate levels of different nutrients such as potassium, some for, phosphorus, zinc and vitamins A and B complex.

There are a number of different clinical studies that have looked at the health benefits of garlic in preventing heart disease.

1. Garlic Lowers Cholesterol

As you will very well know, high cholesterol has been shown to increase the risk of heart disease to an extent. The synthesis of cholesterol takes place in the liver under the influence of an enzyme called hedging giclée reductase. Garlic has been found to contain compounds that can block this enzyme and hence reduce the levels of cholesterol formation in the liver.

2. Garlic Reduces Stickiness Of Blood Cells:

One feature that is common to heart disease is excessive thickness of the blood. The blood cells called platelets can stick together and form a clot which is called a thrombus. Studies have found that regular consumption of garlic can reduce the stickiness of platelets and hence reduce the formation of blood clots within the arteries. Blood clots within the arteries are a common cause of heart attacks.

3. Garlic Controls Blood Pressure:

Extracts of garlic have been found to modulate certain factors that are responsible for controlling blood pressure. High blood pressure is a risk factor in the development of heart disease and controlling blood pressure is essential to protect the heart.

4. Garlic Reduces Oxidative Stress:

Oxidative stress refers to the formation of free radicals that are responsible for damaging the heart arteries leading to heart disease. In one particular study that looked at patients with high blood pressure, garlic pearls were given as a regular supplement. These subjects were found to not only have a decrease in their blood pressure but also had lower levels of oxidative stress. In other words, regular consumption of garlic can protect the heart from various damaging free radicals.

The Indian diet is already rich in garlic. It is used as a common spice in our cooking. Don't throw the garlic away. Instead eat it and reap the benefits of cardiac protection.

4. Ginger:

Again, ginger is a common spice that is used in cuisine in India. It is even added to tea to make 'masala chai'.

The good news about ginger is that it has a number of different cardiovascular benefits that have been demonstrated in clinical studies.

In one particular study that looked at daily ginger consumption, Chinese researchers found that regular consumption of ginger reduced the risk of developing high blood pressure by 8%. In addition to this, they also found that the risk of coronary artery disease also reduced by nearly 13%. The recommended intake of ginger to reap this benefit was 2 to 4 grams per day.

1. Ginger Lowers Cholesterol:

In one study conducted at Babol University Of medical sciences, it was found that regular ginger consumption could reduce the levels of bad cholesterol i.e. LDL cholesterol. In addition to that, it also elevated the levels of good cholesterol i.e. HDL cholesterol. Animal studies found that garlic was as effective as taking a cholesterol-lowering medication when it came to lowering bad cholesterol levels.

2. Ginger Controls Blood Sugars:

Diabetes is an important risk factor in the development of heart disease. High blood sugars are a well-known to damage the blood vessels and cause narrowing of the heart arteries leading to heart attacks and heart failure.

Clinical research has found that using ginger or as a supplement to your daily diet can help reduce fasting blood sugars by almost 12%. In the long term, it is able to lower the blood sugar values by nearly 10%.

Clearly, ginger has a number of different health benefits making it a great herbal remedy to prevent heart disease.

5. Capsicum:

Capsicum contains the active ingredient capsaicin which is responsible for giving it a spicy flavour.

In a clinical study published in 2015, it was found that capsaicin may have a number of different heart benefits.

In particular, it was found that could control blood pressure, lower blood sugar, reduce the strain on the heart muscle and control heart muscle thickness, reduce body weight and slow down atherosclerosis.

Capsaicin also has the property of thinning the blood and preventing it from clotting. This is important in preventing heart attacks.

There are a number of different herbal remedies to prevent heart disease. It is important that you partake in some of these on a regular basis at least.

By combining these herbal remedies with regular exercise and a healthy balanced diet, you can reduce your risk of developing heart attacks and heart failure from a very young age.

Garlic

Garlic is one of several foods that promote liver health. The liver is like the body's own personal filtering system; it has regenerative properties, helps clear out waste and toxins, aids in digestion and keeps the blood healthy. But we don't always treat our livers right (we blame you, mouth-watering sangria). To make sure your liver isn't being overworked, here are seven foods with liver-protecting powers. Incorporate some of them into your diet to naturally cleanse and clean this vital organ!

Grapefruit

Vitamin C could play a role in keeping your liver

healthy; research has indicated it can help people with liver cirrhosis. Just one cup of grapefruit meets the daily vitamin C intake. Just keep in mind that the fruit can also affect drug metabolism. If you're on medications, talk to your doctor before digging into them.

Avocados

In 2000, Japanese researchers reported that avocados, filled with healthy fats, contain phytochemicals that reduced liver damage in rats.

Beets

The research is still in the early stages, but there's some evidence that beets can protect the liver by reducing excess fatty acids.Turmeric

Turmeric has been used in Chinese and Ayurvedic medicine for treating liver problems for centuries, according to the University of Maryland, and research from 2001. It indicated that the curcuminoids found in the spice might prevent fat accumulation in the organ.

Garlic

Thousands of years ago, garlic was prescribed to

treat a wide range of conditions and illnesses, including respiratory problems, parasites and poor digestion. Now, a study published in the Journal of Nutritional Biochemistry, reports garlic supplements may benefit liver function. Another paper found that a garlic-derived compound might help heal alcohol-induced liver damage.

KIDNEY STONES & WAYS TO CLEANSE YOUR KIDNEYS

Highlights

Kidneys make one of the most essential organs of the human body. Their constant healthy functioning is required to ensure the body's smooth mechanism.

After all, kidneys help to detox and filter impurities from the blood, pulling out the waste products, and further regulating the fluid balance in the body. They excrete toxins and excess water to the bladder for elimination as urine.

However, due to various reasons, if the kidneys are not able to excrete these toxins and waste, crystals or unprocessed minerals start to develop, which are known as kidney stones.

Kidney stones may be small or big depending on how grave the situation is. Small kidney stones are easily curable unless you hit the nerve in the initial stages.

There are various symptoms to identify this problem and get it treated on time. Here, we jot down the causes, symptoms and natural cure for kidney stones.

Causes of Kidney Stones

The general causes of kidney stones may include lack of water in the body, production of excessive acidic environment in urine, urinary tract infections, etc. It is curable easily if diagnosed at an early stage.

Symptoms of Kidney Stones

There can be more than one symptom for kidney stones, which include,

- Excessive pain in the abdomen, lower back or urinary tract. The pain can vary from excruciating, sharp or mild depending on the severity.
- Persistent urge to urinate, or even blood in urine.
- Feeling nauseated or severe vomiting
- Constant sweating or chills

The symptoms may vary on the basis of severity. There can be a constant discomfort and pain on the sides, which could further spread down to other parts of the body.

Note: These symptoms may vary from person to person. It is not necessary to witness all these symptoms altogether.

Natural Remedies to Remove Kidney Stones

1. Kidney Beans

Kidney beans that have a close resemblance to that of a kidney, is known to remove kidney stones effectively and cleanse the kidneys. Kidney beans are high on-fibre and are a great source of minerals and B vitamins that help in cleaning your kidneys and help the urinary tract function better.

2. Apple Cider Vinegar

The presence of citric acid in apple cider vinegar helps in dissolving kidney stones, further alkalising blood and urine, and helping to remove the stones. Regular consumption of apple cider vinegar will help in flushing out the unnecessary toxins in the kidney.

3. Pomegranate Juice

The seeds and the juice of pomegranate are important for removing kidney stones as they are a good source of potassium. Potassium prevents the formation of mineral crystals that can develop in to kidney stones. It also reduces the formation of stones due to its astringent properties, flushing out the toxins from the kidney and lowering the acidity levels in the urine.

4. Dandelion Roots

According to our expert Nutritionist and Macrobiotic Health Coach, Shilpa Arora, drinking dandelion root tea (root pulled out of the ground) or dried organic dandelion for tea is good for cleansing kidneys. It acts as a kidney tonic and further stimulates the bile production that carries away the waste and aids in better digestion.

5. Basil

Basil is diuretic in nature and acts as a detoxifier that helps in removing kidney stones and further strengthens its functioning. It lowers uric acid levels in blood, cleansing the kidneys. It consists of acetic acid and other essential oils that help in breaking the stones down to pass through urine. It also acts as a pain killer.

6. Lemon And Olive Oil

While olive oil acts as a smooth passage to let the stone pass through the kidney to the bladder, according to the book Healing Foods by DK Publishing, lemons have the highest concentration of citrate. Consuming dilute lemon juice daily has been shown to decrease the rate of stone formation. The compound hydroxycitrate (HCA) can dissolve calcium oxalate crystals, the most common component for kidney stones.

7. Watermelon

Watermelon consists of high amount of potassium salts that help in regulating the acidic levels in urine. According to the book The Complete Book of Ayurvedic Home Remedies, A Comprehensive Guide to the Ancient Healing of India by Vasant Lad, try drinking a cup of watermelon juice with one fourth teaspoon coriander powder.

Watermelon is a diuretic, so this mixture will give the kidneys a good flushing and help to remove small stones and crystals. Use these two to three times a day.

8. Dates

According to Shilpa Arora, "Dates soaked in water overnight and consumed after taking the seeds out works well for dissolving kidney stones." Dates have a high amount of fibre that helps lower the risk of forming kidney stones. It also consists of magnesium that is responsible for cleansing the kidneys.

According to Shilpa, other remedies also include cherries, cucumber juice and coconut water, which work really well for removing kidney stones. However, we still recommend referring to your doctor before starting to consume these ingredients.

PILES OR HAEMORRHOIDS

Piles or Haemorrhoids can be defined as swellings that develop inside and around the anus. They are cushions of tissue, which consist of blood vessels, muscle and so on.

They are present in varying sizes and could also be outside the anus. It is not considered a serious problem and generally they disappear on their own. However, it is important to note that, sometimes, surgical procedures are required to remove piles.

Generally, genetic factors are associated with piles. They could be inherited. It is believed that as one grows older, the risk of developing piles increases. Pregnant women are more vulnerable to this problem.

Often, it is seen that excessive abdominal pressure causes the veins in the anal area to swell up, transforming into piles. Obesity is a major factor here.

Another important factor, which is often sidelined, is one's diet. Diet is a predominant aspect of our lifestyle and an unhealthy diet could be the result of innumerable health issues, piles being just one of them.

Very often people do not realize that they are suffering from piles. Certain visible symptoms that would help recognize the issue are present.

Pain and bleeding in the anus is very common. Mostly people see the development of a lump or a swelling in the area, which means there are piles. Itching and anal discharge is also common.

Fortunately, the cure of this problem lies no further than your own home. You need not worry as the treatment for piles lies in your hands itself.

*Here are some home remedies
that work wonders in
the case of piles.*

According to BN Sinha, Ayurveda Expert, the sole reason for piles is constipation. It is more common among those who are involved in jobs that require sitting for long hours.

People who do not indulge in any form of exercise and movement of the body are more vulnerable to piles, BN Sinha believes.

Home remedies that work as miracles and could help

improve one's condition naturally, in 2-3 weeks:

1) Triphala Powder –

As mentioned above, constipation is a major cause for piles, triphala powder must be taken regularly to remove constipation and hence prevent piles from developing.

How to use this ingredient? BN Sinha suggests taking 4 grams of triphala powder every night before going to bed, in hot water. It works like magic if one is regular in its intake.

2) Castor Oil –

Castor oil has wide ranging properties like anti-oxidant rich, anti-fungal, anti-bacterial and anti-inflammatory. Hence, this ingredient has the power to decrease the size of the piles and reduce pain in the individual.

BN Sinha advises taking 3ml of castor oil in milk every night. It could also be applied in the affected area. External application and regular intake, works well to alleviate the pain and symptoms of piles.

3) No Heavy Food In Dinner-

Our dietary habits are often the root cause of most of the health issues we are facing today. Elimination of piles requires one to eat foods that would reduce constipation, which is the number one trigger for piles, and reduce pain.

One must make sure not to eat food products that contain too much fibre. Fibre has bulk formation capacities. Hence it must be avoided. Similarly, too many laxatives cause loose stool, which would cause discomfort if one were suffering from piles.

Deep fried food damages hemorrhoids further. They slow down the digestive system causing irregular bowl movement and increasing inflammation. This causes more pain and irritation. Apart from heavy food, spicy food is a big no-no as well. E

specially in case of bleeding piles, they cause excruciating pain and hence must be avoided.

4) Increase In Water Intake-

This is the simplest strategy to cure piles. Adequate intake of water supplemented by a healthy diet results in healthy bowel movement. Drinking good amounts of water prevents constipation and thus piles.

Having 8-10 glasses of water each day, make one's digestive system smooth and regulates it. It is often said that prevention is better than cure, then why not take advantage of this simple strategy and live a healthy lifestyle?

5) Salads-

BN Sinha advises individuals to consume salads like cucumber every day, right after breakfast. Carrot have antioxidant and anti-inflammatory properties, which are beneficial for curing piles. They also include vitamin C and K, which are known to improve vein health.

6) Asafoetida Or Heengc-

BN Sinha urges one to include heeng in their diet. It could be included in the vegetables on a day-to-day basis or dissolved in a glass of water and must be consumed daily.It is an Indian spice used in cooking as well as curing ailments. It improves digestion and hence cures piles.

TOOTH INFECTION

Some natural remedies can help you control tooth pain and help stop tooth infections from getting worse.

The only way to truly get rid of an infection is with antibiotics. However, home remedies for tooth infection can help manage the symptoms and alleviate some of the pain.

If you have a tooth infection you need to see a dentist to assess whether or not you need a root canal and to get prescription antibiotics to make sure that the infection goes away and doesn't cause any more pain or damage to your teeth.

There are some natural remedies that you can use to both help control the pain and help stop the infection from getting worse or spreading while you wait for the infection to die off. Not all of these remedies will work for every person but if you're in pain from an infected tooth they can bring you some relief.

1. Saltwater Rinse

One of the easiest things that you can do to help lessen the pain of a tooth infection and try to stop the spread of an infection is to rinse your mouth with a warm saltwater solution. A saltwater rinse will kill off some of the bacteria in your mouth and irrigate your mouth. It can rinse some of the debris out of your mouth and if you have an abscess it can help break up the pus surrounding the tooth. You can use regular table salt and warm tap water to make a basic saltwater rinse. Just add about ½ a teaspoon of salt to a small cup of warm water and stir it will. Rinse your mouth with for a couple of minutes swishing the solution thoroughly around your mouth and then spit it out.

2. Baking Soda

A tooth abscess home treatment that you probably have in your kitchen right is baking soda. The same baking soda that you keep in the refrigerator to mitigate odour has antibacterial properties. Rinsing your mouth with a solution of baking soda and warm water will help reduce the amount of plaque in your mouth and help relieve pain. If you have an abscess on the side of your tooth or in your gums, you can make a paste of baking soda and water and apply that directly to your tooth or gum instead of using the rinse. If the infection in your tooth is in another part of the tooth, use the rinse.

3. Essential Oils

Essential oils have been used for their medicinal properties for centuries. Essential oils are made from plants that are distilled with water or steam or cold pressed to extract the oil within the plant leaves and stems. Steam distillation is the most common modern method of extracting oil from plants but in earlier centuries they often used cold pressing to make sure that they got the best quality oil.

To use essential oils to alleviate pain and promote healing you should always keep the essential oils in a cool place away from things like spices or food. Put a couple of drops of the essential oil on a cotton ball or cotton swab and then use that to apply the oil to your tooth.

There are many different gentle essential oils that have been proven to have some success treating any number of dental issues including infection like:

- Oregano oil
- Thyme oil
- Clove oil
- Tea Tree oil
- Lavender oil

When you're using essential oils, make sure that you are using pure medicinal grade essential oils. You can find these at any health food store. Some food co-ops also sell them and you can buy them online. Buy from trusted brands that have a reputation for high quality. Double check to make sure that the bottle says that the oil is therapeutic grade essential oil before using it. These days many makers use "natural" oils to do everything from flavour baked goods to make perfume and soaps. Those oils are scent oils not pure essential oils. Those oils have no therapeutic value and can be dangerous if ingested.

4. Herbal Teas

Herbal teas are another time-tested home remedy for many different ailments. You can make your own herbal teas by buying the leaves and stems of various herbs and simply steeping them in hot water to make a tea. However, it will probably be more effective to buy medicinal grade teas that are already made.

High quality therapeutic grade teas will contain a higher quality of herb and a stronger concentration than anything you can buy so they will most likely be more effective. If your teeth are sensitive to heat because of the infection brew the tea, let it steep for up to 15 minutes depending on how string you want it to be, and let it cool to room temperature before you drink it.

Fenugreek a popular tea to help alleviate the symptoms of a tooth infection. Fenugreek has been documented to have medicinal properties although not enough research has been done to prove that those properties are beneficial for tooth infection home treatment. Fenugreek tea is easy to find at most health food stores and even in some grocery stores with an alternative medicine or alternative health food section.

The other recommended tea for a tooth infection is Goldenseal tea. Goldenseal is an herb related to Turmeric and it has many of the same anti-inflammatory and immune boosting properties that Turmeric has. Goldenseal also has natural antibacterial and antibiotic properties for a tooth infection. Drink up to three cups a day to help knock out a tooth infection.

5. Hydrogen Peroxide

Hydrogen peroxide is something almost everyone has in their medicine kit or first aid cabinet. It has many households and first aid uses, but it's best known for preventing infections in cuts and for being an effective mouthwash. This simple first aid staple is one of the best remedies for an infected tooth. To make a Hydrogen Peroxide mouth rinse use a 1:1 ratio or mix equal parts peroxide and warm water then rinse your mouth with that.

6. Garlic

A tooth abscess home remedy that is easy to find and inexpensive to buy is garlic. You may not like the idea of smelling like garlic just because you're trying to treat a tooth but the healing effects of garlic might make the smell worth it. There is a compound in fresh raw garlic called Allicin that may have significant pain relief and antibacterial properties that can reduce or eliminate the infection in a tooth.If you suspect that you have a tooth infection and you can't get to dentist right away, peeling a clove of garlic and gently biting down on it with your infected tooth can help. You will need to leave the piece of garlic against your tooth for a few minutes for it to be effective.

7. Over-The-Counter Pain Killers

You can take over-the-counter painkillers like acetaminophen, naproxen, or aspirin to control the pain and any radiating pain caused by your tooth infection. Just make sure that you don't take more than the recommended dose and that you make sure that they won't have a bad interaction with any medications that you are taking.

8. Coconut Oil Pulling

Oil pulling is a rather controversial practice. Some people say that it helps maintain good dental hygiene and recommend doing it daily. However, there is no evidence that oil pulling has any medicinal benefits for oral health. Coconut oil has some powerful antibacterial properties so it's possible that oil pulling using liquid coconut oil could help lessen the duration of the infection or make the symptoms more manageable.

9. Cold Compress

A cold compress can help if you have a swollen face from tooth infection. Home remedies can help the tooth pain but cold is the best thing to bring down swelling. Most commercially available cold packs don't bend so it can be difficult to get them to sit right on the curves of your face or neck. Instead of a commercial cold pack, you can make your own by wrapping up some ice in a washcloth or towel. Or, you can always dip into the freezer and grab a bag of frozen corn or peas that will stay cold for a long time and fit well into the contours of your face and neck.

10. Aloe Vera Gel

Aloe Vera gel is often used to treat burns and cuts or skin irritations because it has natural antibacterial properties but it is also an effective way to stop the pain of an infected tooth. It can also help heal abscesses in the gums. When you buy Aloe Vera gel to use in your mouth make sure that you are buying food grade Aloe Vera so that it's safe to ingest. You can also use Aloe Vera liquid but the gel is easier to apply to your teeth and gums. Keep the bottle in the refrigerator for extra pain relief. Applying cold Aloe Vera gel to a painful infected tooth or infected gums can give you instant pain relief and the added benefit of fighting infection.

When to call a dentist

A tooth infection happens when bacteria get into the tooth through a cavity, a chip, or a crack. Infections in the teeth can spread to other teeth, your jaw, or your gums. If a tooth infection is left untreated, it can have serious health consequences, so it's important that you see a dentist to treat it promptly if you have the symptoms of a tooth infection.

Natural remedies can help you manage the symptoms of a tooth infection but you still need to see a dentist about the infection. The dentist can take X-rays to determine if you need a root canal and see how bad the damage from the infection is. You may also need a course of antibiotics. You should call a dentist as soon as you suspect that you have an infected tooth.

EYE INFECTIONS

Over a million people in the US suffer from some type of eye infection each year. Most of these infections can be avoided by following proper hygiene.

Also, through correct identification, many can be treated at home.

Bright Side, through this article, will help you identify and treat the 3 most common eye infections, which don't threaten your vision, but can be extremely irritating and painful.

As the adage goes, 'Prevention is better than cure', don't miss our bonus to know how you can avoid getting infected altogether.

Conjunctivitis

Conjunctivitis or pink eye is a highly contagious infection that manifests itself in the form of inflammation of the outer layer of the white part of the eye and the inside of the eyelid.

In almost 65% of cases conjunctivitis gets cured without

treatment in 2 to 5 days and treatment deals only with reducing the itchiness of the eyes.

Symptoms

Allergic conjunctivitis: Red or pink eyes, pain, itching

Viral conjunctivitis: Red eyes, periodic itching, increased tears

Bacterial conjunctivitis: Red or pink eyes, dryness of the eyes and the skin around them, eye discharge that may form a crust while sleeping

Causes: Allergens, Virus (mostly among adults), bacteria (mostly among kids)

Treatment:

1. Use a compress: Soak a soft towel in cold or warm water (depending on your preference) and then wring it out. Apply it to the eyes and let it rest there until the itching subsides. Use separate towels for each eye and use a new towel every time.
2. Use honey: Mix honey and water in equal parts and stir well. Soak cotton balls in it and apply over your eyes. Perform these 2 to 3 times every day until the symptoms subside.

Stye

A stye is a pimple-like red lump formed on the eyelid (both upper and lower). It occurs due to the infection of the oil glands present in the eyelids. It's very painful, but it usually resolves itself in few days or at most in few weeks without any treatment.

Symptoms:

Red, pimple-like inflammation on the eyelid, swelling of the eyelid, irritation of the eye, light sensitivity, blurred vision

Causes: Bacterial infection of the meibomian gland or the gland of Zeis

Treatment:
1. Use a warm compress: Wet a soft towel with warm water, wring it out so that it is not dripping wet. Place it over the eye with stye. Let is stay for 10-15 minutes. Repeat it several times in a day.
2. Use black tea bag: Put a black tea bag over the eye with the stye, but remember not to use hot or warm tea bags. Let it stay for 5-10 minutes.

Blepharitis

Blepharitis is a noncontagious inflammation of the eyelid. Although blepharitis does not threaten the loss of sight, it can in some cases lead to permanent alterations of the eyelid margin.

Symptoms:

Swollen eyelids, red eyes, sticking of eyelids, formation

of dandruff-like flakes on the eyelids, light sensitivity
Causes: Bacterial infection. Skin conditions like dandruff
or rosacea can up the risk of the infection.

Treatment:

1. Warm compress: Soak a towel in warm water, wring it to drain out the excess water. Apply it to the eye and let it stay for 5-10 minutes. After removing, use a moist cotton ball to remove the dandruff-like crust from the eyelid. Repeat several times a day.
2. Use tea bags: Apply warm black tea bags over the eyelid. Keep it over the eyelid and then dispose of the teabag.
3. Consume food with healthy fats: Foods like avocado, nuts, seeds, coconut oil and olive oil can decrease inflammation and help in the healing of the skin.

Bonus: How to prevent eye infections from happening and spreading

1. Maintain proper hygiene: Wash your hands properly before touching your eyes. You can also use hand sanitizers to keep your hands clean.
2. Do not use contaminated or unclean water to wash your eyes.
3. Never share towels, pillows, handkerchiefs, etc.
4. Keep your eye care kit clean, and change it every six months to avoid germs from inhabiting them.

5. Never share your eye care kit with anyone.
6. Keep your eyeglasses and contact lenses clean and never share your cleaner.
7. If your eyes get infected, do not use eye makeup and avoid using contact lenses.

FUNGAL INFECTIONS

Many people suffer from fungal infections at least once in their lives. Poor hygiene, humidity, and warm climate are possible causes of fungal infections. Diaper rash, athlete's foot, jock itch, and oral thrush are some common fungal infections. Many fungi that cause these infections are already becoming resistant to more aggressive forms of medications.

While over the counter medicines and antifungal creams are readily available in the market, most fungal infections respond very positively to home remedies. Let us take a look at some of them.

Causes of Fungal Infections

1. Hot and humid climate, sweating too much or wearing clothes that are damp can result in the development of fungal infections.
2. Compromised immunity due to underlying disease like diabetes, HIV, cancer etc. can cause fungal infections.
3. Living in an unclean environment and not maintaining personal hygiene can cause fungal infections.

4. Wearing dirty clothes like unclean socks and innerwear can lead to fungal infections.
5. Wearing clothes that are too tight can cause sweating, further resulting in the development of fungal infections.
6. Obesity can lead to fungal infections. Moisture can be retained in skin folds, further giving a breeding ground to fungus.
7. Stress can compromise our immunity further leading to fungal infections.
8. Hormonal changes in pregnancy can lead to vaginal infections.

Home Remedies For Fungal Infection are:

Eat Yogurt And Probiotics

Yoghurt and other probiotics have an ample amount of good bacteria that help stave off many fungal infections. These fight off microbes that cause these infections.

Fermented foods are another excellent source of probiotics. If these are not helping, you could use probiotic supplements that have more concentrated dosages of the good bacteria. Read more on the health benefits of yoghurt.

Wash With Soap And Water

Clean the affected area with soap and water twice daily

before you apply any home remedies or any other medication. This will control the spread of infection.

Use Apple Cider Vinegar

Apple cider vinegar has antifungal properties. You could mix two tablespoons in warm water and drink it up or dip a cotton ball in it and dab over your skin. Doing this thrice a day should produce beneficial results. Know more about the health benefits of apple cider vinegar.

Use Tea Tree Oil

Tea tree oil is naturally antifungal and antibacterial. Mix it with any carrier oil like coconut oil or olive oil and dab over the infected area about three to four times a day. This is one of the most effective home remedies to treat fungal infection.

Use Coconut Oil

In its unheated form, even coconut oil works as a potent antifungal agent. Applying it over the skin makes it a good, safe topical medicine. Since it is easy on the skin, it is also useful to treat scalp ringworm. Use over the skin three times a day.

Use Turmeric

Turmeric is a potent antimicrobial and anti-inflammatory spice. Mix with a little water and apply over the infected area. To get benefits in the internal body environment, mix with warm water, or have turmeric tea.

Use Aloe Vera

One of the most time-tested natural remedies to cure any skin infection is aloe vera. It not only treats the infection but also soothes and repairs skin damage. Also, read aloe vera benefits for face and skin.

Garlic

Garlic is one of the most potent antifungal and anti-microbial herbs. Those who eat garlic regularly are less susceptible to fungal infections. Crush a couple of garlic with some olive oil and make a paste. Apply to the infected area for about thirty minutes. Also, read the benefits of garlic for health.

Oregano Oil

Another active antifungal agent is oregano oil. Mix a few drops with any carrier oil and dab on the affected area. You could also take oregano oil capsules orally.

Follow these remedies regularly to achieve the desired results. Check for allergies to essential oils before using them.

Neem Leaves:

Neem leaves have effective antifungal properties and are extremely good for the skin. Washing the infected area with neem water helps in treating fungal infections. To make neem water, boil neem leaves in water for 2 to 3 minutes.

Consuming Foods Rich In Vitamin C:

Vitamin C (Ascorbic acid) boosts our immune system. It protects our body from various infections. A good immune system also helps to treat fungal infections faster.

Baking Soda:

Baking soda is useful in fungal infections like Athletes Foot. Applying baking soda powder on our feet and the inside of our shoes helps to absorb moisture and sweat. It thus prevents the infection from spreading.

Hydrogen Peroxide:

Hydrogen Peroxide helps to cure Athletes Foot. Soaking our feet in a solution made using equal parts of water and hydrogen peroxide effectively kills the fungus causing athlete's foot.

Ginger:

Gingerol present in ginger has potent antifungal properties. Adding ginger to our diet in the form of ginger tea effectively helps to prevent and treat fungal infections like Candida.

You can also follow certain precautions to prevent or treat fungal infections like:

- Always wear clean clothes
- Avoid using harsh detergents to clean clothes
- Avoid wearing clothes that are too tight. Prefer breathable cotton clothes

- Avoid scratching the affected area as it can worsen the infection and also increase the chances of spreading
- Wash the affected area at least 2 to 3 times a day

- Keep the affected area as dry as possible

When to visit a doctor for fungal infections?

- Even after following home remedies, there is no improvement

- The fungal infection worsens or recurs

- The infection starts spreading

- Women who are pregnant

- People suffering from diabetes

- Fungal infection is accompanied by fever or discharge of pus

EARACHE

People may think that earaches are just a minor nuisance, but they can cause debilitating pain. While waiting for medical care or for antibiotics to work, some home remedies can help.

Ear pain can feel unbearable, making it difficult to sleep, eat, or do anything but think about the pain. Many children find it particularly difficult to deal with an earache.

People who are experiencing severe ear pain should always speak to a doctor, especially for the first time. However, there are remedies that people can use at home to relieve less severe earaches, or as a means of reducing pain.

This article explores nine effective home remedies that may help people experiencing ear pain.

Causes of ear pain

An earache can be mild but an ear infection can cause debilitating pain.

Ear infections are the most common cause of ear pain. When the ear becomes infected, inflammation and build-up of pressure cause pain that can be intense.

People with ear infections often have other symptoms, such as sinus pressure or a sore throat because infections from nearby areas may affect the ear. An ear infection can also be a standalone condition. Most ear infections are bacterial, not viral.

Only a doctor can diagnose an ear infection. People should not take antibiotics without a prescription, or assume that symptoms are due to an ear infection.

However, earaches are not always caused by an ear infection.

Other conditions can also cause pain in the ear.

Those include:

- Referred pain: This may be from infections or inflammation elsewhere in the body. For example, a toothache may cause aching pain in the ear.
- Chronic conditions: These include temporomandibular joint (TMJ) dysfunction.
- Skin infections: If they are in or around the ear.
- Allergic reactions: These could be from a range of things, such as soap, shampoo, or earrings.
- Water: This may cause pain if trapped in the ear.
- Pressure: Changes in altitude can affect pressure in the ears. This usually resolves on its own, often with a popping sensation.

If left untreated, ear infections can spread to the jaw and other regions of the body. They may also damage the ear itself and can cause dangerously high fevers.

When symptoms of an ear problem are present and do not resolve on their own within a day or two, people should speak to a doctor.

If the pain is intense, is accompanied by a high fever, or includes hearing loss, people should seek medical attention immediately.

Nine home remedies for earache

If an earache is not severe, or if a person is waiting for medical treatment to take effect, they may wish to try home remedies to relieve pain.

Here are a series of nine effective home remedies for people experiencing ear pain:

1. Over-The-Counter Medication

Anti-inflammatory drugs can help relieve the pain and discomfort.

Non-steroidal anti-inflammatory drugs (NSAID's) can temporarily reduce the pain of an earache. People experiencing ear pain can try:

- ibuprofen

- acetaminophen
- aspirin

It is important to remember that it is not safe to give aspirin to babies and young children. This is because of the risk of a potentially life-threatening condition called Reye's syndrome.

The U.S. Food and Drug Administration (FDA) recommend that parents speak to a doctor before giving over-the-counter drugs to a child under 2 years old.

These drugs can cause serious side effects in babies and young children. Note also that the dosage for children is often significantly lower than the proper dosage for adults.

2. Heat

Heat from an electric heating pad or hot pack can reduce inflammation and pain in the ear.

Apply a hot pad to the ear for 20 minutes. For best results, people should touch the neck and throat with the hot pad.

The heating pad should not be unbearably hot. People should never fall asleep with a heating pad, or allow a child to use a hot pack without adult supervision.

3. Cold

A cold pack can help with the pain of an earache.

Try wrapping ice in paper towels or freezing a cold pack and then covering it with a light cloth. Hold this to the ear and the area immediately under the ear for 20 minutes.

The cold should not hurt, and parents should never apply ice directly to their children's skin.

Some people find that heat offers greater relief than cold. For others, alternating hot and cold packs (20 minutes hot, followed by 20 minutes cold) provides the best pain relief.

4. Ear Drops

Ear drops can reduce pressure in the ear caused by fluid and earwax.

People should read the directions carefully, and talk to a doctor before using ear drops on a child.

Ear drops are no substitute for prescription ear drops or antibiotics, so people should only use them for a few days. If symptoms return, people should see a doctor.

It is important to remember that people should not use ear drops in a child with tubes in their ears or whose eardrum has ruptured.

5. Massage

Gentle massage can help with ear pain that radiates from the jaw or teeth, or that causes a tension headache.

People can massage the tender area, as well as any surrounding muscles. For example, if the area behind the ear hurts, try massaging the muscles of the jaw and neck.

Massage may also help with the pain of an ear infection.

- Using a downward motion, apply pressure beginning just behind the ears and down the neck.
- Continuing to apply pressure downward, work forward to the front of the ears.

This type of massage may help drain excess fluid from the ears, and prevent the pain from getting worse.

6. Garlic

Eating a clove of garlic a day may help prevent ear infections.

Garlic has long been used in folk medicine to relieve pain. Some research suggests it has antimicrobial properties that can fight infection.

People should not use it as a substitute for antibiotics a doctor has recommended. Instead, consider adding garlic to an antibiotic regimen to speed up relief.

To prevent ear infections, try eating a clove of garlic each day.

Garlic ear drops may also reduce pain and prevent an infection from getting worse. Cook two or three cloves in two tablespoons of mustard or sesame seed oil until brown, then strain the mix. Then, apply a drop or two to each ear.

7. Onions

Like garlic, onions can help fight infection and reduce pain. Also like garlic, onions are not a substitute for medical attention.

Heat an onion in the microwave for a minute or two. Then, strain the liquid and apply several drops to the ear. A person may want to lie down for 10 minutes, and then allow the liquid to flow out of the ear. Repeat this as needed.

8. Sucking

Sucking can help reduce pressure in the Eustachian tubes, offering some relief.

Babies who are nursing may feel better when allowed and encouraged to nurse as frequently as possible. Adults and children can suck on hard candy or cough drops.

9. Breast Milk

Breast milk has antimicrobial properties. Some research suggests that a mother's breast milk changes based on the microbes to which a baby is exposed.

This means that breast milk is most effective in babies. However, some sources suggest that breast milk may even help adults. Infants and children should continue nursing to get the most benefits from breast milk.

In nursing babies, as well as in children and adults, topical application of breast milk may also help. Even if it doesn't, breast milk is unlikely to cause any serious side effects.

People can try dropping a few drops of breast milk in each ear, and repeat the application every few hours as needed.

RHEUMATOID ARTHRITIS PAIN RELIEF

You'll need to keep up with your usual medical care, but some natural remedies might help relieve pain and stiffness from rheumatoid arthritis (RA).

Many of them are simple, like using heat and ice packs. Others, like acupuncture, need a trained pro.

If you want to try natural and home remedies, ask your doctor what would be most helpful for you and if there are any limits on what's OK for you to try.

If he gives you the go-ahead, you might want to look into some of these common treatments:

Heat And Cold

Many doctors recommend heat and cold treatments to ease rheumatoid arthritis symptoms. Each offers different benefits:

Cold:

It curbs joint swelling and inflammation. Apply an ice pack to the affected joint during an RA flare-up, for instance. Just don't overdo it. Apply the cold compress for 15 minutes at a time. Take at least a 30-minute break between treatments.

Heat:

It relaxes your muscles and spurs blood flow. You can use a moist heating pad or a warm, damp towel. Many people like using microwaveable hot packs. Don't go too hot. Your skin shouldn't burn.

You can also use heat therapy in the shower. Let the warm water hit the painful area on your body. That may help soothe it. A hot tub is another good way to relax stiff muscles. Just don't use hot tubs or spas if you have high blood pressure, heart disease, or are pregnant.

Magnets

Magnet therapies come in a variety of forms, such as bracelets, necklaces, inserts, pads, or disks. You can find them at most natural food stores.

Most research on magnets involves people with osteoarthritis, the wear-and-tear type of arthritis linked to aging, not RA.

In people with knee and hip osteoarthritis, some early studies have shown they improved joint pain better than a placebo.

Doctors don't know exactly how magnets might relieve pain, and there's no clear proof that they actually help people with rheumatoid arthritis.

Acupuncture

This traditional form of Chinese medicine is one of the oldest natural pain remedies around. It uses super-fine needles to stimulate energy along pathways in your body called meridians.

The goal is to correct imbalances of energy, or qi (pronounced "chee"). There isn't a lot of research specific to RA, although studies do show it lowers levels of chemicals in your body linked to inflammation. It also helps with chronic pain, especially back pain. It may also help with osteoarthritis.

Since it involves needles that need to be clean and properly placed, ask your rheumatologist to recommend a practitioner who works with people that have RA.

Aromatherapy

This natural treatment doesn't appear to affect pain levels or chemicals that cause inflammation. But it might boost your mood. One small study found lemon scent might boost your mood, but that's about it.

Essential oils can be a nice addition to a massage. Be careful if you apply them to your skin or let someone else do it. Some are known irritants. Try a test patch to see how you react. Don't use it on broken or damaged skin.

Biofeedback

This technique helps you learn to control automatic responses such as heart rate and blood pressure. You do it with sensors on your body, which send information to a monitor.

A therapist teaches you how to control your reaction to stresses.

Deep Breathing

Take slow breaths from your belly. It can calm you and turn off the stress receptors that tighten your muscles and make pain worse. Plus, when you focus on your breathing, you take your brain away from thoughts about pain.

Exercise

You may not feel like moving, but it's good for you. It won't make your RA worse, and it could lower the swelling in your joints and help ease your pain.

Talk to your doctor or a physical therapist before you get started. They can help create the right program for you.

It'll probably focus on:

- Aerobics, like walking or swimming, to get your heart moving
- Strength training, to keep the muscles around your joints strong
- Range-of-motion exercises to help your joints move like they should
- Balance moves to help you avoid stumbles and falls

Massage

This natural remedy dates back thousands of years. But modern science does show it can help ease pain. There are many different types. You'll want to talk to your doctor before you try it.

You can also ask for recommendations. It's good to get a massage therapist who's worked with people that have RA. Let him know if you have any sore spots he needs to avoid.

You can also ask him not to use scented products that could irritate your skin.

Meditation

This technique can be as simple as focusing on your breathing and just noticing each inhale and exhale. It doesn't require any spiritual beliefs, and it isn't about being super-calm.

Anyone can do it, and only a few minutes can make a difference. Your mind will almost certainly wander.

That's OK. Just return your attention to your breath, or whatever else you choose to focus on.

Progressive Muscle Relaxation

To do this:

- Tighten and then relax the muscles in different parts of your body.
- Work your way down the body, starting with your face muscles, followed by your neck, arms, chest, back, belly, legs, and feet. Or work your way up from your feet.
- Breathe in as you contract your muscles.
- Breathe out when you let go.

Tai Chi

This slow, gentle martial art is easy on your joints. You'll stand and do a series of gentle movements that are easy to modify if your joints are sore.

It can help with strength, flexibility, and balance. There isn't enough research to know if it works to curb RA pain, but it may be something to try.

Thunder God Vine

A few studies have shown a drop in inflammation and tender joints in people with RA who take this supplement. This includes some studies which compared this root with sulfasalazine, a traditional drug used to treat RA, and found that symptoms improved more with the use of thunder god vine. Side effects may include stomach upset, headache, hair loss, upper respiratory tract infections, and sterility in men. Pregnant women and women at risk of getting osteoporosis should not take it.

Topical Creams, Gels, And Patches

You might not think of a pain rub as a natural remedy, but many of these products are made from capsaicin, the ingredient that makes chili peppers hot. Studies show it can help ease RA pain. Don't use it along with a heating pad. It makes burns more likely.

Turmeric

This golden spice found in many curries is a member of the ginger family. It hails from India and Indonesia and has been a staple in traditional medicine in that part of the world for centuries.

Research shows it blocks proteins that cause inflammation and may ease pain as well as some nonsteroidal anti-inflammatory drugs (NSAIDs) commonly used to treat RA.

Visualization

This can help reduce stress and pain. To try this simple exercise:

- Close your eyes.
- Breathe deeply.
- Picture yourself in a quiet, peaceful place.

Yoga

This mix of low-impact exercise, breathing, and meditation was developed in India some 5,000 years ago. It's good for your body and mind. It can ease joint pain, improve your flexibility, and zap stress and tension. Studies show it can lower chemicals that cause inflammation and stress. Just talk to your doctor to make sure it's OK for you before you dive in. Work with them to find an instructor that knows how to handle people with RA.

Tell your doctor about anything you take, even if it's natural, so he can check that it's safe for you.

SINUS INFECTION AND SINUSITIS

Sinusitis is an inflammation of the sinuses, and can be either chronic (lasting 8-12 weeks or longer) or acute (lasting less than 4 weeks). There are many causes of sinusitis and sinus pain, including viral and bacterial sinus infections – but it can also be caused by other sources of inflammation, including allergies.

Approximately 1 in 10 people will experience a sinus infection at some point in their lifetime, and the pain associated with it can be debilitating and greatly impact one's quality of life.

Symptoms can include congestion, pain or pressure in the face, nasal discharge or post-nasal drip, as well as a reduced ability to smell. Patients likely won't have a fever.

While common treatments for sinusitis include antibiotics and even surgery in extreme cases, you don't need to resort to such drastic measures if you prefer a more natural route. There are many natural remedies for sinus infections and sinus pain, including the ones below.

Note that the information below is no replacement for a doctor's advice, and if you are unsure or your illness or treatment options, you should always consult with your physician first.

1. Enjoy A Cuppa Something Hot

Turns out grandma's chicken noodle soup is good for more than simply soothing the soul, so go ahead and enjoy a cup of the good stuff.

"The hot steam from the soup may be its chief advantage, although laboratory studies have actually reported that ingredients in the soup may have anti-inflammatory effects."

2. Grapefruit Seed Extract

A natural antibiotic, grapefruit seed extract can help to clear mucus and prevent other microbial contaminants from taking up residence in your nasal passages.

"GSE is a strong natural antibiotic and works really well against fungus also."

3. Salt Water Rinse

Using a Neti pot or over-the-counter nasal irrigation system can help clear sinuses and relieve symptoms associated with a sinus infection while flushing any bacteria out. "Saltwater washes (saline lavage or irrigation) help keep the nasal passages open by washing out thick or dried mucus.

They can also help improve the function of cilia that

help clear the sinuses. This can help prevent the spread of infection to the other sinuses and reduce postnasal drip. It also can make the nose feel more comfortable by keeping the mucous membranes moist."

4. Steam

Hold your face over a bowl of hot water with a few drops of essential oil – peppermint and eucalyptus are especially effective – to help relieve congestion from sinusitis. Running a hot shower and breathing in the steam is also effective. "Boil a pot of water and remove it from the stove. Add 3 or 4 drops of tea tree oil. Cover your head and pot with a towel and inhale (as much as you can). You will need to inhale for 5 to 10 minutes."

5.Skip The Booze

Alcohol, especially beer, has an inflammatory effect in the body, and that includes in the nasal passages. Frequent or over-consumption of alcohol can exacerbate sinus pain. "It is amazing how even casual consumption of alcohol can cause nasal and sinus membranes to swell, exposing them to irritation and infection."

6. Pressure Points

Acupressure, or other manual manipulation of the sinus areas (performed by a trained osteopath) is a natural remedy that can help relieve sinus pressure and congestion in a matter of minutes. "Believe it or not, a simple 5 minute face massage that you can do yourself, anywhere, will bring you the much needed (yet temporary) relief from your blocked nose – Without medication."

7. Clear The Mucus

Removing excess mucous can help relieve irritation and reduce inflammation in the sinuses. Not to mention you'll be breathing easier. "Even with one inhale of this warming pungent drink, you'll be able to breathe through your nose and feel less cloudy in your head." –

8. Hydrate, Hydrate, Hydrate

Drinking plenty of water and other fluids can help clear mucus from your nasal cavities and help drain from your sinuses. "Patients with sinusitis should drink plenty of fluids to avoid dehydration. Water, which helps lubricate the mucous membranes, is the best fluid to drink."

9. Turn Up The Heat

We've all experienced it – that head-clearing sensation that occurs when we eat a really spicy dish – it can clear even the most stubborn of sinuses. "Spicy foods that contain hot peppers or horseradish may help clear sinuses."

10. Turmeric

A powerful anti-inflammatory, turmeric is a natural remedy that can help relieve inflammation in the sinuses caused by a nasty sinus infection. "The active ingredient in turmeric, known as curcumin, helps to heal the sinus cavity and clear the airways. Since sinus infections are caused by nasal inflammation, and turmeric possesses anti-inflammatory properties, the spice can be an effective solution for sinus infection." Mike Barrett

11. Apple Cider Vinegar

A cureall for many things that ail you, apple cider vinegar can help thin congestion associated with sinusitis. "Acv thins the mucus to clear sinuses. Apple cider vinegar helps to deliver a number of nutrients to the body that supports overall immune system and prevents infection. Once the infection has developed, the substance in ACV helps to dilute and used as rinse to thin the mucus almost immediately and to eliminate the infection very soon. It acts as both nasal rinse and nutritional supplement." Home Remedies for Life

12. Avoid The Pool

Inhaling chemicals like the chlorine at the local swimming pool can irritate the nasal passages, so steer clear if you find it irritates your sinuses. "Sinusitis-prone people may be uncomfortable in a chlorine treated swimming pool as it irritates the lining of the nose and sinuses."

13. Breathe Deep

Breathing techniques associated with mindfulness-based practices such as yoga, meditation and hypnotherapy can help to relieve the pain associated with sinus infections. "These practices rely on the mind's ability to influence pain perception and are especially helpful with chronic or recurrent pain that is often seen with sinus pressure." Chris Iliades, MD, Everyday Health,

14. Oregano Oil

Given its status as a powerful antifungal and antimicrobial, using oregano oil as a natural home remedy may help relieve or resolve problems associated with sinusitis. "Use of oregano oil in vapor form is one of the best options to cure sinusitis. Mix 2 to 3 drops of oregano oil with half a cup of boiling water. Cover your head and cup with a towel to trap the steam and breathe to inhale it. This will help to clear the nasal passages." Snehal Motkar, Buzzle,

15. Change Your Diet

Certain foods can be particularly irritating for those suffering from a sinus infection, including dairy, gluten and sugar. Cutting these foods from your diet can often help resolve or lessen symptoms of sinusitis. "Cutting out dairy products can also improve sinusitis symptoms as they encourage mucus production." Anastasia Stephens,

16. Sleep With Your Head Elevated

Sleeping with your head elevated – either propped up with extra pillows or with leg extenders attached to your bedframe – can help to drain the sinuses and relieve any symptoms you might be experiencing. "Sleep propped up on pillows or semi-upright in a chair, or raise the head of your bed by using leg extenders." Sandra

Ketcham,

17. Fermented Cod Liver Oil

Rich in vitamins A and D, plus Omega-3 fatty acids, fermented cod liver oil can help clarify skin conditions, and remedy autoimmune disorders – including the chronic inflammation associated with sinusitis. "Furthermore, the primary benefit of fermented cod liver oil is the concentrated presence of naturally occurring fat-soluble vitamins: A, D, E and K2 that are scarce in modern diets." Diane Sanfilippo,

18. Minimize Outdoor Airborne Irritants

Outdoor air irritants like smoke, smog and car exhaust can't always be avoided, but by limiting your exposure to them, you can help reduce sinusitis pain. "You may assume that staying indoors is the best solution in avoiding harmful fumes from the outdoors; however, did you know your sinuses could be exposed to even more harmful irritants inside your very own home?"

19. Treat Indoor Airborne Irritants

Pollen, smoke, dust mites, pet dander – all of these airborne pollutants can contribute to sinus irritation and make your sinus infection even worse. One way to treat this is by installing an air purifier in your home to remove any pollutants. "Just put the purifier on your nightstand and keep it on the whole night. Works wonders!"

20. Supplement Smart

Adding certain natural supplements into your daily diet can help relieve symptoms and address any nutritional shortfalls that might be contributing to your sinusitis pain. "Vitamin C and Vitamin B6 help prevent inflammation and excessive histamine levels while zinc strengthens overall immunity."

21. Reintroduce Moisture Into Your Home

Dry air, especially during the winter-time, can exacerbate any symptoms you're feeling from sinus infections. Running a humidifier can help take the edge off some of the dryness in your home and help you breathe easier. "Air-conditioning and dry-air heating systems can cause sinus irritation and dryness, which can potentially increase eye puffiness in the morning."

22. Break A Sweat

Much like exercise can help in other aspects of your health and contribute to general well-being, so too can it help prevent and relieve symptoms of sinusitis. So step away from the TV and computer and take a stroll around the block. "Developing and adhering to a weekly exercise routine is a necessity when it comes to maintaining healthy sinuses."

23. Hot Compress

One simple, natural technique for relieving pressure and pain associated with sinusitis is to alternate applying warm and cold compresses to the nasal passages. "Place a hot compress across your sinuses for three minutes, and then a cold compress for 30 seconds. Repeat this procedure three times per treatment, two to six times a day."

24. Hum A Little Tune

As strange as it may sound, research out of Sweden found that humming can help to clear sinuses and reduce your chances of developing a sinus infection. "Humming increases both airflow through your sinuses and the level of nitric oxide in your sinuses. The combination of nitric oxide and airflow may reduce your risk of sinusitis." Chris Iliades

25. Butt Out

Multiple studies have shown that smoking causes irritation to the nasal passages, and butting out can help reduce that irritation almost instantly. "Tobacco and smog are famous for causing irritation of the sinus lining which causes bad drainage of mucus."

26. Wash Your Hands

One of the most common causes of sinusitis is bacterial

and viral infections, and frequent, proper hand washing is one of the best ways to reduce the spread of germs, so wash well and wash often – especially during cold and flu season. "You can help prevent problems in your sinuses by practicing good hygiene. For example, wash your hands before eating and after using the bathroom. Be cognizant of what you touch during the day. Make sure to wash your hands before touching your face." Brindles Lee Macon

27. Eat Well

The best offence is a good defence, and that's true when it comes to preventing and healing from sinusitis. Eating a diet that's high in fruits and vegetables can help boost your immune system. "A nutritious diet can not only decrease inflammation in your system, but also boost your immunity to bacteria that can lead to sinus infections."

28. Garlic

Full of powerful antiviral components, garlic is considered a nutritional powerhouse and used by people in many cultures for its curative properties. "As sinus is a bacterial infection, garlic helps to destroy the bacterial infection and cures the sinus problem." – HomeRemediesforLife

29. Horseradish

With as much kick as hot sauce and other spicy foods, horseradish is a natural remedy that can help to clear any blockages associated with your sinus infection. "The traditional treatment for sinusitis is to "take a half tea-spoonful of grated horseradish sauce without dilution both morning and afternoon. Do not drink anything or eat for at least ten minutes after the dose."" Life Extension Magazine.

30. Lemon Balm

An herb used in many medicinal treatments, lemon balm can help kill bacteria that cause or worsen symptoms of sinus infections. "You can boil some dried lemon balm leaves for about ten minutes. Then sieve the mixture and use the water to gargle. It provides great relief from sinus congestion." Sanchita Chowdhury, BoldSky.

NECK AND SHOULDER PAIN

Along with other types of chronic pain, neck and shoulder pain can be treated with a combination of natural therapies and healthy practices. Hot and cold therapy, stretching and strengthening exercises, and healthy posture are top recommendations.

Hot, cold and electrotherapy

Heating pads, ice or cold packs, and electrotherapy are natural ways to get relief from neck and shoulder pain. A general rule of thumb suggests choosing different therapies based on how long you've been experiencing pain.

Use Cold For Recent Neck Or Shoulder Pain

During the first six weeks after a fresh injury, experts recommend applying ice to help reduce inflammation and pain. Ice packs, cold sprays, and/or cold gels are great options to relieve acute swelling.

Use Heat For Chronic Aches And Pains

Heat encourages blood flow and helps relax tight muscles. This type of therapy can be introduced six weeks after an injury, and also works best for lingering aches and pains. Make sure your heat therapy isn't too hot. Try:

- Heating pads
- Heating packs
- Hot towels
- Warm baths, whirlpools and saunas
- Warm baths with Epsom salts

Try Electrotherapy For Short And Long-Term Neck And Shoulder Pain

TENS, or Transcutaneous Electrical Nerve Stimulation, is a drug-free alternative to pain relief that works for both short- and long-term pain. TENS units use mild, pain-free electrical currents to disrupt pain signals.

Make sure you don't place the TENS unit pads too close to your head or sides of your neck and spine. Please follow the manufacturer's directions for the best and safest pad placement.

*Stretching and strengthening
for neck and shoulder pain*

Stretching and strengthening help relieve pain and also

build up muscle support to prevent future injuries. These gentle exercises should not make you feel any additional pain, so if they do, stop right away and consult a healthcare professional.

Stretches For Neck Pain

Here are three simple stretches to relieve neck pain.

1. Lower your chin to your chest while keeping your shoulders straight. Hold the stretch for 15 to 30 seconds. Relax and slowly lift your chin back to the starting position.

2. Rotate your head to one side while keeping your shoulders straight. Hold for 15 to 30 seconds. Relax and slowly return to the first position. Repeat on the other side.

3. Tilt your head so that you're moving your ear toward your shoulder. Hold for 15 to 30 seconds. Relax and slowly return to the first position. Tilt your head to the other side and repeat.

*Use these stretches as a warm up
to your strengthening exercises.*

Strengthening Exercises For Neck Pain

Here are two exercises to help prevent future neck pain and injuries:

Squeeze your shoulder blades together and hold for 5 seconds. Don't squeeze too hard; it should feel comfortable. Repeat 10 times twice a day.

Keeping your neck in a neutral position, do a wall push-up with your feet shoulder-width apart and your elbows straight. Repeat 10 times with 1 to 2 sets. Do this twice a day.

Stretching Exercises For Shoulder Pain

These stretching exercises help loosen up the tight muscles that cause pain and can improve flexibility to prevent future injuries.

Move your chin forward, then slowly pull it back toward your throat, tucking slightly. Keep your chin parallel to the floor. Do this up to 10 times hourly.

Stand upright with a slight bend to your upper back. Now roll your shoulders up, back and down in a fluid circle. Do this 10 times, and then switch directions and roll your shoulders forward 10 times.

Use these stretches as a warm up to your strengthening exercises.

Strengthening Exercises For Shoulder Pain

These are two examples of strengthening exercises that help prevent shoulder pain using little to no equipment.

- Fill a water bottle (1.5 liters or so) about ¾ full
- Keeping your arm straight, hold the bottle in front of you at shoulder height for 30 to 60 seconds
- Switch arms, doing this 3 times on each side

- Lie on your stomach with your arms at your sides. Put a pillow under your forehead if you need to
- Gently bring your shoulder blades together and toward your feet
- Relax your shoulders about halfway down and hold for 10 seconds
- Release your shoulders and repeat the exercise 10 times

You can also prevent neck and shoulder pain by working on your posture.

Adjusting your posture to prevent neck and shoulder pain

It might not be obvious, but posture has a cascading effect on other parts of the body. Paying attention to your core strength and lower back can ease strain on your neck and shoulders.

Check Your Standing Posture

Take the wall test to adjust your standing posture.

- Stand with your head, shoulder blades, and buttocks touching the wall
- Keep your heels around 2 to 4 inches away from

the wall
- Put your hand behind the curve in your back and touch the wall with your palm

Your hand should fit neatly inside of this space.
- If the fit is too loose, tighten your abdominal muscles
- If it's too tight, arch your back

Remember what it feels like when you find the right spot. This is the standing posture you want to maintain as much as possible. Do the wall test daily as many times as you need to.

Adjust Your Sitting Posture

If you spend a lot of time behind a desk, fixing your sitting posture is especially important.
- Avoid crossing your legs
- Keep your feet flat with your ankles in front of your knees
- Make sure your feet touch the floor or use a foot-rest
- Relax your shoulders so they're not too rounded or pulled backwards
- Keep your elbows close to your sides and bent at about 90 degrees
- Unlike standing posture, make sure your whole back touches the chair. Use a back pillow if you need to
- Make sure your thighs and hips are supported with a well-padded seat

- Keep your thighs and hips parallel to the floor

Make sure to take breaks from sitting by adjusting your position, taking brief walks, and stretching your muscles.

Maintaining good health and well-being requires taking care of your whole body. The causes and cures for neck and back pain are no exception to the rule. Remember, if pain persists or you are unsure that you may have an injury, consult a healthcare professional.

Herbs to Fight Arthritis Pain

- Aloe Vera
- Boswellia
- Cat's Claw
- Eucalyptus
- Ginger
- Green Tea
- Thunder God Vine
- Turmeric
- Willow Bark
- Other options
- Ask a Doctor

Overview

There are different types of arthritis, but they can all cause pain. Some natural remedies may help you manage mild symptoms, particularly if you use them alongside other treatment options.

Certain herbs may have anti-inflammatory properties that can help with rheumatoid arthritis (RA) or osteo-arthritis (OA).

Still, there's a lack of scientific evidence to support the use of many of these options, and some may have negative effects.

Before opting for "natural" remedies for arthritis, be sure to talk to a doctor first, as some options may interact with existing medications.

1. Aloe Vera

Aloe vera is one of the most commonly used herbs in alternative medicine. It's available in many forms, such as pills, powder, gels, and as a leaf.

Known for its healing properties, it's popular for treating small skin abrasions, such as sunburn, but it may also help with joint pain.

Possible benefits include Source the following:

- It has anti-inflammatory properties.
- It doesn't have the negative gastrointestinal effects of nonsteroidal anti-inflammatory drugs (NSAIDs), commonly used for arthritis pain.

Topical application: You can apply a gel directly to the skin.

Oral medication: Some researchers have suggested that taking aloe by mouth may help relieve osteoarthritis pain.

More studies are needed to confirm that these treatments are beneficial.

The National Centre for Complementary and Integrative Health (NCCIH) notes that aloe vera use is likely to be safe, but some people have side effects when they take it by mouth.

It may lower glucose levels and interact with some diabetes medications.

2. Boswellia

Practitioners of traditional and alternative medicine use Boswellia serrata, also called frankincense, for its anti-inflammatory properties. It's derived from the gum of Boswellia trees, which are indigenous to India.

According to a review published in 2011, boswellic acid appears to have anti-inflammatory effects that could help people with RA, OA, and gout.

Results from human trials have suggested that frankincense capsules may help improve pain, function, and stiffness due to OA. However, these were small studies. More research is needed.

Doses of up to 1 gram a day of boswellia appear to be safe, but high doses can affect the liver. It's available in tablet form and topical creams.

3. Cat's Claw

Cat's claw is another anti-inflammatory herb that may reduce swelling in arthritis. It comes from the bark and root of a tropical vine that grows in South and Central America.

People have traditionally used it as an anti-inflammatory and to boost the immune system.

The Arthritis Foundation notes that, like many conventional drugs for rheumatoid arthritis, cat's claw suppresses tumor necrosis factor (TNF).

They cite a small 2002 study in which cat's claw was shown effective in reducing joint swelling by over 50 percent in 40 people with RA.

However, possible side effects include:

- nausea and dizziness
- low blood pressure
- headache

You shouldn't use this herb if you:

- use blood thinners
- take medications that suppress the immune system
- have tuberculosis

According to the NCCIH, some small studies have looked at cat's claw for rheumatoid arthritis, but more research is needed.

4. Eucalyptus

Eucalyptus is a readily available remedy that people use for a wide range of conditions. Extracts of eucalyptus leaves feature in topical remedies to treat arthritis pain.

The plant leaves contain tannins, which may help reduce swelling and pain related to arthritis. Some people follow up with heat pads to maximize the effect.

Eucalyptus aromatherapy may help ease the symptoms of RA.

Always dilute an essential oil with a carrier oil before use. Use 15 drops of oil with 2 tablespoons of almond or another neutral oil.

Be sure to test yourself for allergies before using topical eucalyptus, which is referred to as a patch test.

Put a small amount of the product on your forearm. If there's no reaction in 24 to 48 hours, it should be safe to use.

5. Ginger

Many people use ginger in cooking, but it may also have medicinal benefits. The same compounds that give ginger its strong flavour also have anti-inflammatory properties, studies have found.

Some researchers say ginger could one day be an alternative to nonsteroidal anti-inflammatory drugs (NSAIDs).

People have long used ginger in traditional medicine to treat nausea, but you can also use it for rheumatoid arthritis, osteoarthritis, and pain in the joints and muscles.

The authors of one 2016 review article believe that, in the future, ingredients in ginger could form the basis of a pharmaceutical treatment for rheumatoid arthritis. It could not only help manage symptoms but also help prevent bone destruction.

Here Are Some Ways Of Consuming Ginger:

- Make tea by infusing tea bags or fresh ginger in boiling water for 5 minutes.
- Add powdered ginger to baked goods.
- Add powdered ginger or fresh ginger root to savoury dishes.
- Grate fresh ginger onto a salad or stir fry.

Check with a doctor before increasing your intake of ginger, as it can interfere with some medications, such as warfarin (Coumadin), a blood thinner.

6. Green Tea

Green tea is a popular beverage. The antioxidants it contains may help fight the inflammation that occurs with.

You can take green tea as:

- a beverage

- powder (matcha) for sprinkling on food or adding to smoothies
- supplements

While scientists have found evidence that extracts or specific components of green tea may have an effect on arthritis, it's unclear whether the concentration of active ingredients in a cup of tea will help relieve symptoms.

That said, it's likely to be safe for most people. As a beverage, it is a healthier option than some coffees, soda, and other sweetened drinks, as long as you don't add sugar.

More research is needed to confirm that green tea can help reduce inflammation and to find out which form and dose would be most effective.

You can find a selection of green tea options online.

7. Thunder God Vine

Thunder god vine (Tripterygium wilfordii) is an herb. It has long been used in Chinese, Japanese, and Korean medicine to manage inflammation and excessive immune activity.

This could make it a suitable treatment for rheumatoid arthritis and other autoimmune diseases.

You can use it:

- by mouth, as a dietary supplement
- as a topical treatment, applied directly to the

skin

However, it can have very serious negative effects, such as:

- gastrointestinal problems
- respiratory infections
- hair loss
- headache
- a skin rash
- menstrual changes
- changes in sperm that could reduce fertility in males
- after 5 years or more of use, there may be a reduction in bone density

Many medications can interact with thunder god vine, especially those commonly used for RA and other autoimmune diseases.

Extracts from the wrong part of the vine can be toxic. With this in mind, it's also important to remember that the Food and Drug Administration (FDA) doesn't regulate the production or sale of natural remedies.

You can't always be sure exactly what a product contains, and if thunder god vine herb is prepared incorrectly, it can be deadly.

The NCCIH says there's not enough evidence to prove that thunder god vine is safe or effective for treating arthritis.

It's important to talk to your doctor about this herb.

There are other treatment options available that have been shown to be effective with less risk.

8. Turmeric

Turmeric is a yellow powder made from a flowering plant. It adds flavour and colour to sweet and savory dishes and teas.

Its main ingredient, curcumin, has anti-inflammatory properties. It has long played a role in traditional Ayurvedic and Chinese medicine. It may help with OA, RA, and other arthritic conditions.

Turmeric is available:

- as a powdered spice to add to dishes
- in tea bags
- as supplements that are taken by mouth

More studies into the safety and effectiveness of turmeric are needed. The NCCIH notes that it's likely safe for most adults, although high doses or long-term use may result in gastrointestinal upset.

Purchase turmeric supplements online.

9. Willow Bark

Willow bark is an ancient treatment for pain and inflammation. You can use it either as a tea or in tablet form.

Some research says it may help relieve joint pain related

to OA and RA. However, results have been conflicting, and more studies are needed. Also, it may not be safe for everyone.

Common side effects include:

- stomach upset
- high blood pressure
- an allergic reaction, especially if you have an allergy to aspirin
- stomach ulcers and bleeding in the case of an overdose

You should ask your doctor before using willow bark, especially if you're using blood thinners or have a stomach ulcer. Do not take it if you're allergic to aspirin.

Can diet play a role in treating osteoarthritis? Find out here.

Ask your doctor about complementary medicine

As interest in herbal medicine grows, conventional doctors have become more willing to assess the benefits of alternative remedies.

When treating arthritis, some herbs may complement your current medications. But it's important to understand that herbs can cause serious side effects.

Buying herbal treatments from a reputable source is also essential.

The FDA doesn't monitor herbs for quality, purity, packaging, or dosage, so there's no way of knowing if a product is contaminated or contains inactive ingredients.

Discuss all arthritis treatment options with your doctor and don't stop taking prescribed medications unless they recommend it.

GET RID OF TRAPPED GAS

Gas trapped in the intestines can be incredibly uncomfortable. It may cause sharp pain, cramping, swelling, tightness, and even bloating.

Most people pass gas between 13 and 21 times a day. When gas is blocked from escaping, diarrhoea or constipation may be responsible.

Gas pain can be so intense that doctors mistake the root cause for appendicitis, gallstones, or even heart disease.

20 ways to get rid of gas pain fast

Most people pass gas between 13 and 21 times a day, but diarrhoea and constipation can block the gas from escaping.

Luckily, many home remedies can help to release trapped gas or prevent it from building up. Twenty effective methods are listed below.

1. Let It Out

Holding in gas can cause bloating, discomfort, and pain. The easiest way to avoid these symptoms is to simply let out the gas.

2. Pass Stool

A bowel movement can relieve gas. Passing stool will usually release any gas trapped in the intestines.

3. Eat Slowly

Eating too quickly or while moving can cause a person to take in air as well as food, leading to gas-related pain.

Quick eaters can slow down by chewing each bite of food 30 times.

Breaking down food in such a way aids digestion and can prevent a number of related complaints, including bloating and indigestion.

4. Avoid Chewing Gum

As a person chews gum they tend to swallow air, which increases the likelihood of trapped wind and gas pains.

Sugarless gum also contains artificial sweeteners, which

may cause bloating and gas.

5. Say No To Straws

Often, drinking through a straw causes a person to swallow air. Drinking directly from a bottle can have the same effect, depending on the bottle's size and shape.

To avoid gas pain and bloating, it is best to sip from a glass.

6. Quit Smoking

Whether using traditional or electronic cigarettes, smoking causes air to enter the digestive tract.

Because of the range of health issues linked to smoking, quitting is wise for many reasons.

7. Choose Non-Carbonated Drinks

Carbonated drinks, such as sparkling water and sodas, send a lot of gas to the stomach. This can cause bloating and pain.

8. Eliminate Problematic Foods

Carbonated drinks such as sparkling waters and soda send a lot of gas to the stomach, which can cause bloating and pain.

Eating certain foods can cause trapped gas. Individuals find different foods problematic.

However, the foods below frequently cause gas to build up:

- artificial sweeteners, such as aspartame, sorbitol, and maltitol
- cruciferous vegetables, including broccoli, cabbage, and cauliflower
- dairy products
- fibre drinks and supplements
- fried foods
- garlic and onions
- high-fat foods
- legumes, a group that includes beans and lentils
- prunes and prune juice
- spicy foods

Keeping a food diary can help a person to identify trigger foods. Some, like artificial sweeteners, may be easy to cut out of the diet.

Others, like cruciferous vegetables and legumes, provide a range of health benefits. Rather than avoiding them entirely, a person may try reducing their intake or preparing the foods differently.

9. Drink Tea

Some herbal teas may aid digestion and reduce gas pain fast. The most effective include teas made from:

- anise
- chamomile
- ginger
- peppermint

Anise acts as a mild laxative and should be avoided if diarrhoea accompanies gas. However, it can be helpful if constipation is responsible for trapped gas.

10. Snack On Fennel Seeds

Fennel is an age-old solution for trapped wind. Chewing on a teaspoon of the seeds is a popular natural remedy.

However, anyone pregnant or breast-feeding should probably avoid doing so, due to conflicting reports concerning safety.

11. Take Peppermint Supplements

Peppermint oil capsules have long been taken to resolve issues like bloating, constipation, and trapped gas. Some research supports the use of peppermint for these symptoms.

Always choose enteric-coated capsules. Uncoated capsules may dissolve too quickly in the digestive tract, which can lead to heartburn.

Peppermint inhibits the absorption of iron, so these capsules should not be taken with iron supplements or by people who have anemia.

12. Clove Oil

Clove oil has traditionally been used to treat digestive complaints, including bloating, gas, and indigestion. It may also have ulcer-fighting properties.

Consuming clove oil after meals can increase digestive enzymes and reduce the amount of gas in the intestines.

13. Apply Heat

When gas pains strike, place a hot water bottle or heating pad on the stomach. The warmth relaxes the muscles in the gut, helping gas to move through the intestines. Heat can also reduce the sensation of pain.

14. Address Digestive Issues

People with certain digestive difficulties are more likely to experience trapped gas. Those with irritable bowel syndrome (IBS) or inflammatory bowel disease, for example, often experience bloating and gas pain.

Addressing these issues through lifestyle changes and medication can improve the quality of life.

People with lactose intolerance who frequently experience gas pain should take greater steps to avoid lactose or take lactase supplements.

15. Add Apple Cider Vinegar To Water

Apple cider vinegar aids the production of stomach acid and digestive enzymes. It may also help to alleviate gas pain quickly.

Add a tablespoon of the vinegar to a glass of water and drink it before meals to prevent gas pain and bloating. It is important to then rinse the mouth with water, as vinegar can erode tooth enamel.

16. Use Activated Charcoal

Activated charcoal is a natural product that can be bought in health food stores or pharmacies without a prescription. Supplement tablets taken before and after meals can prevent trapped gas.

It is best to build up the intake of activated charcoal gradually. This will prevent unwanted symptoms, such as constipation and nausea.

One alarming side effect of activated charcoal is that it can turn the stool black. This discolouration is harmless and should go away if a person stops taking charcoal supplements.

17. Take Probiotics

Gentle exercises can relax the muscles in the gut, and yoga poses can be especially beneficial after meals.

Probiotic supplements add beneficial bacteria to the gut. They are used to treat several digestive complaints, including infectious diarrhoea.

Some research suggests that certain strains of probiotics can alleviate bloating, intestinal gas, abdominal pain, and other symptoms of IBS.

Strains of Bifidobacterium and Lactobacillus are generally considered to be most effective.

18. Exercise

Gentle exercises can relax the muscles in the gut, helping to move gas through the digestive system. Walking or doing yoga poses after meals may be especially beneficial.

19. Breathe Deeply

Deep breathing may not work for everyone. Taking in too much air can increase the amount of gas in the intestines.

However, some people find that deep breathing techniques can relieve the pain and discomfort associated with trapped gas.

20. Take An Over-The-Counter Remedy

Several products can get rid of gas pain fast. One popular medication, simethicone, is marketed under the following brand names:

- Gas-X
- Mylanta Gas
- Phazyme

Anyone who is pregnant or taking other medications should discuss the use of simethicone with a doctor or pharmacist.

LOWER YOUR BLOOD SUGAR LEVELS

High blood sugar occurs when your body can't effectively transport sugar from blood into cells.

When left unchecked, this can lead to diabetes.

Here are some easy ways to lower blood sugar levels naturally:

1. Exercise Regularly

Regular exercise can help you lose weight and increase insulin sensitivity.

Increased insulin sensitivity means your cells are better able to use the available sugar in your bloodstream.

Exercise also helps your muscles use blood sugar for energy and muscle contraction.

If you have problems with blood sugar control, you

should routinely check your levels. This will help you learn how you respond to different activities and keep your blood sugar levels from getting either too high or too low (2).

Good forms of exercise include weight lifting, brisk walking, running, biking, dancing, hiking, swimming and more.

BOTTOM LINE:

Exercise increases insulin sensitivity and helps your muscles pick up sugars from the blood. This can lead to reduced blood sugar levels.

2. Control Your Carb Intake

Your body breaks carbs down into sugars (mostly glucose), and then insulin moves the sugars into cells.

When you eat too many carbs or have problems with insulin function, this process fails and blood glucose levels rise.

However, there are several things you can do about this.

Some studies find that these methods can also help you plan your meals appropriately, which may further improve blood sugar control .

Many studies also show that a low-carb diet helps reduce blood sugar levels and prevent blood sugar spikes .

What's more, a low-carb diet can help control blood sugar levels in the long run.

BOTTOM LINE:

Carbs are broken down into glucose, which raises blood sugar levels. Reducing carbohydrate intake can help with blood sugar control.

3. Increase Your Fibre Intake

Fibre slows carb digestion and sugar absorption. For these reasons, it promotes a more gradual rise in blood sugar levels.

Furthermore, the type of fibre you eat may play a role.

There are two kinds of fibre: insoluble and soluble. While both are important, soluble fibre specifically has been shown to lower blood sugar levels.

Additionally, a high-fibre diet can help manage type 1 diabetes by improving blood sugar control and reducing blood sugar lows.

Foods that are high in fibre include vegetables, fruits, legumes and whole grains.

The recommended daily intake of fibre is about 25 grams for women and 38 grams for men. That's about 14 grams for every 1,000 calories.

BOTTOM LINE:

> *Eating plenty of fibre can help with blood sugar control, and soluble dietary fibre is the most effective.*

4. Drink Water And Stay Hydrated

Drinking enough water may help you keep your blood sugar levels within healthy limits.

In addition to preventing dehydration, it helps your kidneys flush out the excess blood sugar through urine.

One observational study showed that those who drank more water had a lower risk of developing high blood sugar levels.

Drinking water regularly re-hydrates the blood, lowers blood sugar levels and reduces diabetes risk

Keep in mind that water and other non-caloric beverages are best. Sugar-sweetened drinks raise blood glucose, drive weight gain and increase diabetes risk

BOTTOM LINE:

> *Staying hydrated can reduce blood sugar levels and help prevent diabetes. Water is best.*

5. Implement Portion Control

Portion control helps regulate calorie intake and can lead to weight loss.

Consequently, controlling your weight promotes healthy blood sugar levels and has been shown to reduce the risk of developing type 2 diabetes.

Monitoring your serving sizes also helps reduce calorie intake and subsequent blood sugar spikes.

Here are some helpful tips for controlling portions:

- Measure and weigh portions.
- Use smaller plates.
- Avoid all-you-can-eat restaurants.
- Read food labels and check the serving sizes.
- Keep a food journal.
- Eat slowly.

BOTTOM LINE:

The more control you have over your serving sizes the better control you will have over your blood sugar levels.

6. Choose Foods With A Low Glycaemic Index

The glycaemic index was developed to assess the body's blood sugar response to foods that contain carbs.

Both the amount and type of carbs determine how a food affects blood sugar levels.

Eating low-glycaemic-index foods has been shown to reduce long-term blood sugar levels in type 1 and type 2 diabetics.

Although the glycaemic index of foods is important, the amount of carbs consumed also matters.

Foods with a low glycaemic index include seafood, meat, eggs, oats, barley, beans, lentils, legumes, sweet potatoes, corn, yams, and non-starchy vegetables.

BOTTOM LINE:

> *It's important to choose foods with a low glycaemic index and watch your overall carb intake.*

7. Control Stress Levels

Stress can affect your blood sugar levels.

Hormones such as glucagon and cortisol are secreted during stress. These hormones cause blood sugar levels to go up.

One study showed that exercise, relaxation and meditation significantly reduced stress and lowered blood sugar levels for students.

Exercises and relaxation methods like yoga and mindfulness-based stress reduction can also correct insulin secretion problems in chronic diabetes.

BOTTOM LINE:

Controlling stress levels through exercise or relaxation methods such as yoga will help you control blood sugars.

8. Monitor Your Blood Sugar Levels

"What gets measured gets managed."

Measuring and monitoring blood glucose levels can also help you control them.

For example, keeping track helps you determine whether you need to make adjustments in meals or medications.

It will also help you find out how your body reacts to certain foods.

Try measuring your levels every day, and keeping track of the numbers in a log.

BOTTOM LINE:

Checking your sugars and maintaining a log every day will help you adjust foods and medications to decrease your sugar levels.

9. Get Enough Quality Sleep

Getting enough sleep feels great and is necessary for good health.

Poor sleeping habits and a lack of rest also affect blood sugar levels and insulin sensitivity. They can increase appetite and promote weight gain.

Sleep deprivation decreases the release of growth hormones and increases cortisol levels. Both of these play an important role in blood sugar control.

Furthermore, good sleep is about both quantity and quality. It is best to get a sufficient amount of high-quality sleep every night.

BOTTOM LINE:

> *Good sleep helps maintain blood sugar control and promote a healthy weight. Poor sleep can disrupt important metabolic hormones.*

10. Eat Foods Rich In Chromium And Magnesium

High blood sugar levels and diabetes have also been linked to micronutrient deficiencies.

Examples include deficiencies in the minerals chromium and magnesium.

Chromium is involved in carb and fat metabolism. It also helps control blood sugar levels, and a lack of chromium may predispose you to carb intolerance.

However, the mechanisms behind this are not completely known. Studies also report mixed findings.

Two studies of diabetes patients showed that chromium had benefits for long-term blood sugar control. However, another study showed no benefits.

Chromium-rich foods include egg yolks, whole-grain products, high-bran cereals, coffee, nuts, green beans, broccoli and meat.

Magnesium has also been shown to benefit blood sugar levels, and magnesium deficiency has been linked to a higher risk of developing diabetes.

In one study, people with the highest magnesium intake had a 47% lower risk of becoming diabetic.

However, if you already eat plenty of magnesium-rich foods, then you probably will not benefit from supplements.

Magnesium-rich foods include dark leafy greens, whole grains, fish, dark chocolate, bananas, avocados and beans.

BOTTOM LINE:

Eating foods rich in chromium and magnesium on a regular basis can help prevent deficiencies and reduce blood sugar problems.

11. Try Apple Cider Vinegar

Apple cider vinegar has many benefits for your health.

It promotes lower fasting blood sugar levels, possibly by decreasing its production by the liver or increasing its use by cells.

What's more, studies show that vinegar significantly influences your body's response to sugars and improves insulin sensitivity.

To incorporate apple cider vinegar into your diet, you can add it to salad dressings or mix 2 teaspoons in 8 ounces of water.

However, it's important to check with your doctor before taking apple cider vinegar if you are already taking medications that lower blood sugar.

BOTTOM LINE:

> *Adding apple cider vinegar to your diet can help your body in many ways, including reducing blood sugar levels.*

12. Experiment With Cinnamon Extract

Cinnamon is known to have many health benefits.

For one, it has been shown to improve insulin sensitivity

by decreasing insulin resistance at the cellular level.

Studies show cinnamon can also lower blood sugar levels by up to 29%.

It slows the breakdown of carbs in the digestive tract, which moderates the rise in blood sugar after a meal.

Cinnamon also acts in a similar way as insulin, although at a much slower rate.

An effective dose is 1–6 grams of cinnamon per day, or about 0.5–2 teaspoons.

BOTTOM LINE:Cinnamon has been shown to reduce fasting blood sugar levels and improve insulin sensitivity.

13. Try Berberine

Berberine is the active component of a Chinese herb that's been used to treat diabetes for thousands of years.

Berberine has been shown to help lower blood sugar and enhance the breakdown of carbs for energy

What's more, berberine may be as effective as some blood sugar lowering drugs. This makes it one of the most effective supplements for those with diabetes or pre-diabetes

However, many of the mechanisms behind its effects are still unknown. Additionally, it may have some side effects. Diarrhoea, constipation, flatulence and abdominal pain have been reported .

A common dosage protocol for berberine is 1,500 mg per day, taken before meals as 3 doses of 500 mg.

> *BOTTOM LINE:Berberine works well for lowering blood sugar levels and can help manage diabetes. However, it may have some digestive side effects.*

14. Eat Fenugreek Seeds

Fenugreek seeds are a great source of soluble fibre, which can help control blood sugar levels.

Many studies have shown that fenugreek can effectively lower blood sugar in diabetics. It also helps reduce fasting glucose and improve glucose tolerance .

Although not that popular, fenugreek can easily be added to baked goods to help treat diabetes. You can also make fenugreek flour or brew it into tea .

Fenugreek seeds are also considered one of the safest herbs for diabetes .

The recommended dose of fenugreek seeds is 2–5 grams per day.

BOTTOM LINE:Consider giving fenugreek seeds a try. They are easy to add to your diet and can help regulate blood glucose levels.

15. Lose Some Weight

It's a no-brainer that maintaining a healthy weight will improve your health and prevent future health problems.

Weight control also promotes healthy blood sugar levels and has been shown to reduce your risk of developing diabetes.

Even a 7% reduction in body weight can decrease your risk of developing diabetes by up to 58%, and it seems to work even better than medication.

What's more, these decreased risks can be sustained over the years.

You should also be conscious of your waistline, as it is perhaps the most important weight-related factor for estimating your diabetes risk.

A measurement of 35 inches (88.9 cm) or more for women and 40 inches (101.6 cm) or more for men is associated with an increased risk of developing insulin resistance, high blood sugar levels and type 2 diabetes.

Having a healthy waist measurement may be even more important than your overall weight.

BOTTOM LINE:

> *Keeping a healthy weight and waistline will help you maintain normal blood sugar levels and decrease your risk of developing diabetes.*

Take Home Message

Make sure to check with your doctor before making lifestyle changes or trying new supplements.

This is particularly important if you have problems with blood sugar control or if you are taking medications to lower your sugar levels.

PARALYSIS

1.Mustard Oil

Mustard Oil is very effective in curing paralysis. Apply Mustard oil on the affected part of the body. You can also use Ghee in place of mustard oil.

Yoga

Anulom Vilom Asana has very positive results in paralysis. Practice it continuously for 1 hour and you will see the immediate results as well. It is the best way to cure Paralysis. It has the ability to cure paralysis within 2 weeks. Kapalbhati, Ujjai Pranayama are also very effective.

Acupressure

Press the ring finger upper part to get relief in paralysis. If paralysis is on left side. Press left ring finger and vice versa.

Garlic

Garlic is also another effective home remedy to cure paralysis. Take 5 to 6 pieces of Garlic and grind them. Now add two spoons of honey in it. Now take this mixture daily and within two months, you can get relief from paralysis. Also boil 5–6 pieces of garlic in the milk and take them on daily. This will control your blood pressure as well as affected part will also become alive.

Kalonji Oil (Nigella Sativa Oil)

In this method lukewarm the Kalonji oil and massage it lightly on the affected part of the body. Also take two to three spoons of Kalonji Oil on daily. Within 30–45 days you will see the positive change in the condtion.

Black Pepper (Kali Mirch)

It is another effective way to cure paralysis. In this method take 50–60 grams of black pepper and cook it in the 250 ml Mustard Oil. Now lukewarm this cooked oil and apply it gently on the affected part. This will provide you relief in short period of time.

Ginger

Ginger is very useful in curing paralysis. Take 5 gram of Grinded ginger along with 10 grams of Urad Dal (split black gram). Now, cook it in 50 grams of mustard oil for 10 minutes. Also add 2 grams of powdered camphor in it. Now use this mix oil to massage gently on the affected area. You will experience the surprising relief within few days. This oil is also beneficial in Arthritis.

LOWER YOUR BLOOD PRESSURE

High blood pressure is a dangerous condition that can damage your heart. It affects one in three people in the US and 1 billion people worldwide .

If left uncontrolled, high blood pressure raises your risk of heart disease and stroke.

But there's good news. There are a number of things you can do to lower your blood pressure naturally, even without medication.

Here are 15 natural ways to combat high blood pressure.

1. Walk And Exercise Regularly

Regular exercise can help lower your blood pressure.

Exercise is one of the best things you can do to lower high blood pressure.

Regular exercise helps make your heart stronger and more efficient at pumping blood, which lowers the pressure in your arteries.

In fact, 150 minutes of moderate exercise, such as walking, or 75 minutes of vigorous exercise, such as running, per week, can help lower blood pressure and improve your heart health.

What's more, doing even more exercise than this reduces your blood pressure even further, according to the National Walkers' Health Study.

Bottom line: Walking just 30 minutes a day can help lower your blood pressure. More exercise helps reduce it even further.

2. Reduce Your Sodium Intake

Salt intake is high around the world. In large part, this is due to processed and prepared foods.

For this reason, many public health efforts are aimed at lowering salt in the food industry.

Many studies have linked high salt intake with high blood pressure and heart events, including stroke.

However, more recent research indicates that the relationship between sodium and high blood pressure is less clear.

One reason for this may be genetic differences in how people process sodium. About half of people with high blood pressure and a quarter of people with normal levels seem to have a sensitivity to salt.

If you already have high blood pressure, it's worth cutting back your sodium intake to see if it makes a differ-ence. Swap out processed foods with fresh ones and try seasoning with herbs and spices rather than salt.

Bottom line: Most guidelines for lowering blood pressure recommend reducing sodium intake. How-ever, that recommendation might make the most sense for people who are salt-sensitive.

3. Drink Less Alcohol

Drinking alcohol can raise blood pressure. In fact, alco-hol is linked to 16% of high blood pressure cases around the world.

While some research has suggested that low-to-moder-ate amounts of alcohol may protect the heart, those benefits may be offset by adverse effects.

In the U.S., moderate alcohol consumption is defined as no more than one drink a day for women and two for men. If you drink more than that, cut back.

Bottom line: Drinking alcohol in any quantity may raise your blood pressure. Limit your drinking in line with the recommendations.

4. Eat More Potassium-Rich Foods

Potassium is an important mineral.

It helps your body get rid of sodium and eases pressure on your blood vessels.

Modern diets have increased most people's sodium intake while decreasing potassium intake.

To get a better balance of potassium to sodium in your diet, focus on eating fewer processed foods and more fresh, whole foods.

Foods that are particularly high in potassium include:

- vegetables, especially leafy greens, tomatoes, potatoes, and sweet potatoes
- fruit, including melons, bananas, avocados, oranges, and apricots
- dairy, such as milk and yogurt
- tuna and salmon
- nuts and seeds
- beans

Bottom line: Eating fresh fruits and vegetables, which are rich in potassium, can help lower blood pressure.

5. Cut Back On Caffeine

If you've ever downed a cup of coffee before you've had your blood pressure taken, you'll know that caffeine causes an instant boost.

However, there's not a lot of evidence to suggest that drinking caffeine regularly can cause a lasting increase .

In fact, people who drink caffeinated coffee and tea tend to have a lower risk of heart disease, including high blood pressure, than those who don't drink it.

Caffeine may have a stronger effect on people who don't consume it regularly.

If you suspect you're caffeine-sensitive, cut back to see if it lowers your blood pressure.

> *Bottom line: Caffeine can cause a short-term spike in blood pressure, although for many people, it does not cause a lasting increase.*

6. Learn To Manage Stress

Listening to soothing music may help lower stress.

Stress is a key driver of high blood pressure.

When you're chronically stressed, your body is in a constant fight-or-flight mode. On a physical level, that means a faster heart rate and constricted blood vessels.

When you experience stress, you might also be more likely to engage in other behaviors, such as drinking alcohol or eating unhealthful food that can adversely affect blood pressure.

Several studies have explored how reducing stress can help lower blood pressure. Here are two evidence-based tips to try:

- Listen to soothing music: Calming music can help relax your nervous system. Research has shown it's an effective complement to other blood pressure therapies (21, 22).
- Work less: Working a lot, and stressful work situations, in general, are linked to high blood pressure (23, 24).

Bottom line: Chronic stress can contribute to high blood pressure. Finding ways to manage stress can help.

7. Eat Dark Chocolate Or Cocoa

Here's a piece of advice you can really get behind.

While eating massive amounts of dark chocolate probably won't help your heart, small amounts may.

That's because dark chocolate and cocoa powder are rich in flavonoids, which are plant compounds that cause blood vessels to dilate.

A review of studies found that flavonoid-rich cocoa improved several markers of heart health over the short term, including lowering blood pressure.

For the strongest effects, use non-alkalized cocoa powder, which is especially high in flavonoids and has no added sugars.

Bottom line: Dark chocolate and cocoa powder contain plant compounds that help relax blood vessels, lowering blood pressure.

8. Lose Weight

In people with overweight, losing weight can make a big difference to heart health.

According to a 2016 study, losing 5% of your body mass could significantly lower high blood pressure .

In previous studies, losing 17.64 pounds (8 kilograms) was linked to lowering systolic blood pressure by 8.5 mm Hg and diastolic blood pressure by 6.5 mm Hg .

To put that in perspective, a healthy reading should be less than 120/80 mm Hg .

The effect is even greater when weight loss is paired with exercise.

Losing weight can help your blood vessels do a better job of expanding and contracting, making it easier for the left ventricle of the heart to pump blood.

Bottom line: Losing weight can significantly lower high blood pressure. This effect is even more significant when you exercise.

9. Quit Smoking

Among the many reasons to quit smoking is that the habit is a strong risk factor for heart disease.

Every puff of cigarette smoke causes a slight, temporary increase in blood pressure. The chemicals in tobacco are also known to damage blood vessels.

Surprisingly, studies haven't found a conclusive link between smoking and high blood pressure. Perhaps this is because smokers develop a tolerance over time.

Still, since both smoking and high blood pressure raise the risk of heart disease, quitting smoking can help lessen that risk.

Bottom line: There's conflicting research about smoking and high blood pressure, but what is clear is that both increase the risk of heart disease.

10. Cut Added Sugar And Refined Carbs

There's a growing body of research showing a link between added sugar and high blood pressure.

In the Framingham Women's Health Study, women who drank even one soda per day had higher levels than those who drank less than one soda per day.

Another study found that having one less sugar-sweetened beverage per day was linked to lower blood pressure.

And it's not just sugar — all refined carbs, such as the kind found in white flour — convert rapidly to sugar in your bloodstream and may cause problems.

Some studies have shown that low carb diets may also help reduce blood pressure.

One study on people undergoing statin therapy found that those who went on a 6-week, carb-restricted diet saw a greater improvement in blood pressure and other heart disease markers than people who did not restrict carbs.

Bottom line: Refined carbs, especially sugar, may raise blood pressure. Some studies have shown that low carb diets may help reduce your levels.

11. Eat Berries

Berries are full of more than just juicy flavour.

They're also packed with polyphenols, natural plant compounds that are good for your heart.

Polyphenols can reduce the risk of stroke, heart conditions, and diabetes, as well as improving blood pressure, insulin resistance, and systemic inflammation.

One study assigned people with high blood pressure to a low-polyphenol diet or a high-polyphenol diet containing berries, chocolate, fruits, and vegetables.

Those consuming berries and polyphenol-rich foods experienced improved markers of heart disease risk.

Bottom line: Berries are rich in polyphenols, which can help lower blood pressure and the overall risk of heart disease.

12. Try Meditation Or Deep Breathing

While these two behaviors could also fall under "stress reduction techniques," meditation and deep breathing deserve specific mention.

Both meditation and deep breathing may activate the parasympathetic nervous system. This system is engaged when the body relaxes, slowing the heart rate, and lowering blood pressure.

There's quite a bit of research in this area, with studies showing that different styles of meditation appear to have benefits for lowering blood pressure (36, 37).

Deep breathing techniques can also be quite effective.

In one study, participants were asked to either take six deep breaths over the course of 30 seconds or simply sit still for 30 seconds. Those who took breaths lowered their blood pressure more than those who just sat (38).

Try guided meditation or deep breathing. Here's a video to get you started.

Bottom line: Both meditation and deep breathing can activate the parasympathetic nervous system, which helps slow your heart rate and lower blood pressure.

13. Eat Calcium-Rich Foods

People with low calcium intake often have high blood pressure.

While calcium supplements haven't been conclusively shown to lower blood pressure, calcium-rich diets do seem linked to healthful levels.

For most adults, the calcium recommendation is 1,000 milligrams (mg) per day. For women over 50 and men over 70, it's 1,200 mg per day.

In addition to dairy, you can get calcium from collard greens and other leafy greens, beans, sardines, and tofu.

> *Bottom line: Calcium-rich diets are linked to healthy blood pressure levels. You can get calcium through eating dark leafy greens and tofu, as well as dairy.*

14. Take Natural Supplements

Some natural supplements may also help lower blood pressure. Here are some of the main supplements that have evidence behind them:

- Aged garlic extract: Researchers have used aged

garlic extract successfully as a stand-alone treatment and along with conventional therapies for lowering blood pressure (42, 43).

- Berberine: Traditionally used in Ayurvedic and Chinese medicine, berberine may increase nitric oxide production, which helps decrease blood pressure (44, 45).

- Whey protein: A 2016 study found that whey protein improved blood pressure and blood vessel function in 38 participants (46).

- Fish oil: Long credited with improving heart health, fish oil may benefit people with high blood pressure the most (47, 48).

- Hibiscus: Hibiscus flowers make a tasty tea. They're rich in anthocyanins and polyphenols that are good for your heart and may lower blood pressure (49).

Bottom line: Researchers have investigated several natural supplements for their ability to lower blood pressure.

15. Eat Foods Rich In Magnesium

Magnesium is an important mineral that helps blood vessels relax.

While magnesium deficiency is pretty rare, many people don't get enough.

Some studies have suggested that getting too little magnesium is linked with high blood pressure, but evidence from clinical studies has been less clear.

Still, eating a magnesium-rich diet is a recommended way to ward off high blood pressure .

You can incorporate magnesium into your diet by consuming vegetables, dairy products, legumes, chicken, meat, and whole grains.

Bottom line: Magnesium is an essential mineral that helps regulate blood pressure. Find it in whole foods, such as legumes and whole grains.

Take home message

High blood pressure affects a large proportion of the world's population.

While drugs are one way to treat the condition, there are many other natural techniques, including eating certain foods that can help.

Controlling your blood pressure through the methods in this article may, ultimately, help you lower your risk of heart disease.

URIC ACID

Presence of high uric acid in bloodstream can cause gout. To prevent this condition, it is essential to watch your eating habits. A healthy eating and proper medication could help you maintain uric acid at normal levels.

Below are some of the foods that you must add in your diet to keep uric acid at normal levels...

Apples

Add apples in your diet. As they are enriched with malic acid, they neutralize uric acid in blood stream. This gives relief to the patients who are suffering from high uric acid condition.
Apple cider vinegar

Intake of apple cider vinegar is also beneficial for people suffering with high uric acid. You can add 3 teaspoons of vinegar to 1 glass of water. You can have it 2-3 times every day. Drinking apple cider vinegar helps in treating high uric acid condition.

French Bean Juice

Drinking extracted juice of French beans is an effective home remedy to treat gout. This healthy juice should be consumed twice a day as it prevents the production of high uric acid in blood.

Water

Another reason to have adequate water throughout the day. Water helps in flushing out toxins from the body including excess presence of uric acid. So have at least 8-9 glasses of water every day.

Cherries

As they have anti-inflammatory substance referred to as anthocyanins, it helps in reducing uric acid levels. They also prevent uric acid from crystallizing and getting deposited in the joints. Another reason you should have cherries is they neutralize the acids and help in preventing inflammation and pain.

Berries

Consume berries, especially strawberries and blueberries. Enriched with anti-inflammatory properties, including them in your diet is beneficial to prevent high uric acid levels in blood.

Fresh Vegetable Juices

Have carrot juice and add beetroot juice and cucumber juice in it. This is an effective remedy to treat high uric acid in blood.

Low Fat Dairy Products

Another way to treat high uric acid is by consuming low fat dairy products in your diet. Go for low fat milk and curd and prevent high uric acid in blood.

Lime

As lime juice contains citric acid, a solvent of uric acid, adding it to your daily diet is helpful in preventing high uric acid level. Squeeze half a lime juice in a glass of water and have it every day.

Vitamin C Enriched Foods

Including foods enriched with vitamin C is another way to maintain uric acid levels. These foods disintegrate uric acid and flushes it out of the body. Include foods such as kiwi, amla, guava, kiwi, oranges, lemon, tomato and other green leafy vegetables.

Olive Oil

Cook your foods with cold-pressed olive oil. This is a healthy start as it contains anti-oxidants and anti-inflammatory properties.

Celery Seed

One of the most popular home remedies to treat high uric acid levels is by consuming celery seeds.

Pinto Beans

Pinto beans are loaded with folic acid which helps in lowering uric acid naturally. You can also eat sunflower seeds and lentils to reduce the risk of high levels of uric acid.

High-Fibre Foods

Adding foods that are high in dietary fibre also helps in lowering uric acid levels in blood. They absorb uric acid from the bloodstream and helps in eliminating excess uric acid from your body through kidneys. If you have been diagnosed with high uric acid, increase the consumption of dietary soluble fibres such as oats, apples, oranges, broccoli, pears, strawberries, blueberries, cucumbers, celery, carrots and barley.

Bananas

Have bananas as including them in your diet is beneficial in lowering excess uric acid levels.

Green Tea

Another way to treat high uric acid is by consuming green tea every day. This helps in controlling hyperuricemia or high uric acid levels and also lowers the risk of developing gout.

Grains

Have grains that are more alkaline. You can consume jowar and bajra.

Tomatoes, Cucumbers And Broccoli

Have tomatoes, cucumbers and broccoli before you start your meal. This is the best way to can prevent the formation of high uric acid in your blood. Their alkaline nature is helpful to maintain uric acid in bloodstream.

Omega 3

Add omega 3 fatty acids. You can have flax-seeds, fish such as salmon, mackerel, herring, sardines and walnuts as they help in reducing swelling and inflammation!

Things to avoid

Sugary Foods And Beverages

While high uric acid is usually linked with a protein-rich diet, recent studies have shown that sugar can also be a potential cause. Most common added sugar include table sugar, con syrup and high fructose corn syrup.

Fructose particularly leads to high levels of uric acid. It's best to check food labels for sugar before buying.

Prefer eating more whole foods and lesser refined packaged to cut down on sugar intake.

Avoid Alcohol

Have you noticed that when you consume alcohol, your trips to the loo increase? Alcohol makes you dehydrated and triggers high uric acid. This happens as your kidney is busy in filtering out the products in the blood due to alcohol instead of uric acid and other wastes.

Manage Your Insulin Levels

Too much insulin in the body can lead to high levels of uric acid and weight gain. It's best to get your insulin levels checked when you visit your doctor, even if you do not have diabetes mellitus.

LOWER YOUR TRIGLYCERIDES

The importance of a clean diet

Do you know how to manage your triglyceride level?

These fatty type of lipids, found in your blood, can be burned away in the process of losing weight, but they can also be dangerous for your health. Similar to LDL (the bad form of cholesterol), high levels of triglycerides can increase the risk of heart disease and stroke, even when LDL levels are regulated.

"We are increasingly recognizing that elevated triglycerides represent a major issue and should not be ignored," says cardiologist Steven Nissen, MD.

You are what you eat

Similar to cholesterol, triglycerides come from the food we eat and our liver. When levels are normal, triglycerides are used for energy. The problems arise when levels are high, explains Dr. Nissen. When we make more triglycerides than we use, the rest are stored as fat. That's why many people who are overweight or type 2 diabetes have high levels.

"Poor diabetes control is a major factor in causing high triglyceride levels," Dr. Nissen says. He stresses the importance of watching your carbohydrate consumption. "Eating a low-carb diet and getting plenty of exercise are often effective in lowering triglyceride levels."

Is there such a thing as good carbs?

Different carbohydrate-loaded foods also contain very different nutritional levels.

Dr. Nissen recommends scaling back or eliminating:

- Refined grains.
- Flour.
- White rice.
- Starchy vegetables (like white potatoes).

"It's particularly important to reduce the consumption of sugar and foods with high-fructose corn syrup," he says.

Foods that contain good carbs and plenty of fibre include:

- Beans.
- Oatmeal.
- Apples (with skin).
- Pears.
- Greens.
- Sweet potatoes.

- Whole grains.
- Brown rice.

Dr. Nissen advises that increasing your fibre intake may lower triglyceride levels. "If you have high triglyceride levels, there's a good chance you don't ingest close to the recommended 25 to 30 grams of fibre a day," he says.

Weight gain isn't just from food

High triglyceride levels can be caused by excessive alcohol consumption as well. So if your levels are higher than normal, it might be a good idea to eliminate alcohol completely.

"Weight has a profound impact on triglycerides," says Dr. Nissen. "If you lose as little as 5 to 10% of body weight, your triglycerides can drop as much as 20%."

VITAMIN B12

Vitamin B12 is an essential nutrient that your body can't make on its own, so you need to get it from your diet or supplements.

Vegetarians, pregnant or breastfeeding women, and others at risk of deficiency may want to track their diets closely to make sure they're getting enough.

What is vitamin B12?

This water-soluble vitamin has many essential functions in your body.

It's necessary for keeping your nerves healthy and supporting the production of DNA and red blood cells, as well as maintaining normal brain function.

Vitamin B12 is absorbed in the stomach with the help of a protein called intrinsic factor. This substance binds to the vitamin B12 molecule and facilitates its absorption into your blood and cells.

Your body stores excess vitamin B12 in the liver, so if you consume more than the RDI, your body will save it for future use.

You may develop a vitamin B12 deficiency if your body

does not produce enough intrinsic factor, or if you don't eat enough vitamin-B12-rich foods.

Vitamin B12 is mainly found in animal products, especially meat and dairy products. Luckily for those on vegans diets, fortified foods can be good sources of this vitamin, too.

Below are 12 healthy foods that are very high in vitamin B12.

1. Animal Liver And Kidneys

Organ meats are some of the most nutritious foods out there. Liver and kidneys, especially from lamb, are rich in vitamin B12.

A 3.5-ounce (100-gram) serving of lamb liver provides an incredible 3,571% of the Daily Value (DV) for vitamin B12.

While lamb liver is generally higher in vitamin B12 than beef or veal liver, the latter two may still contain about 3,000% of the DV per 3.5 ounces (100 grams).

Lamb liver is also very high in copper, selenium, and vitamins A and B2.

Lamb, veal, and beef kidneys are also high in vitamin B12. Lamb kidneys provide about 3,000% of the DV per 3.5-ounce (100-gram) serving. They also provide more than 100% of the DV for vitamin B2 and selenium.

SUMMARY

A 3.5-ounce (100-gram) serving of lamb, beef, or veal liver contains up to 3,500% of the DV for vitamin B12, while the same serving of kidneys contains up to 3,000% of the DV.

2. Clams

Clams are small, chewy shellfish that are packed with nutrients.

This mollusk is a lean source of protein and contains very high concentrations of vitamin B12. You can get more than 7,000% of the DV in just 20 small clams.

Clams, especially whole baby clams, also provide great amounts of iron, with almost 200% of the DV in a 100-gram (3.5-ounce) serving of small clams.

Clams have also been shown to be a good source of anti-oxidants.

Interestingly, the broth of boiled clams is also high in vitamin B12. Canned broth has been shown to provide 113–588% of the DV per 3.5 ounces (100 grams).

SUMMARY

A 3.5-ounce (100-gram) serving of clams contains up to 99 mcg of vitamin B12, which is 4,120% of *the DV.*

3. Sardines

Sardines are small, soft-boned saltwater fish. They're usually sold canned in water, oil, or sauces, though you can also buy them fresh.

Sardines are super nutritious because they contain virtually every single nutrient in good amounts.

A 1-cup (150-gram) serving of drained sardines provides 554% of the DV for vitamin B12.

Furthermore, sardines are an excellent source of omega-3 fatty acids, which have been shown to provide many health benefits, such as reducing inflammation and improving heart health.

SUMMARY

One cup (150 grams) of drained sardines contains up to 500% of the DV for vitamin B12.

4. Beef

Beef is an excellent source of vitamin B12.

One grilled flat iron steak (about 190 grams) provides 467% of the DV for vitamin B12 ().

Also, the same amount of steak contains reasonable amounts of vitamins B2, B3, and B6, as well as more than 100% of the DVs for selenium and zinc.

If you're looking for higher concentrations of vitamin B12, it's recommended to choose from low fat cuts of meat. It's also better to grill or roast it instead of frying. This helps preserve the vitamin B12 content.

SUMMARY

A 3.5-ounce (100-gram) serving of beef contains about 5.9 mcg of vitamin B12. That's 245% of the DV.

5. Fortified Cereal

This source of vitamin B12 may work well for vegetarians and vegans, as it's synthetically made and not derived from animal sources.

Although not commonly recommended as part of a healthy diet, fortified cereals can be a good source of B vitamins, especially B12. Food fortification is the process of adding nutrients that are not originally in the food.

For instance, Malt-O-Meal Raisin Bran offer up to 62% of the DV for vitamin B12 in 1 cup (59 grams).

The same serving of this cereal also packs 29% of the DV for vitamin B6 and good amounts of vitamin A, folate, and iron.

Research shows that eating fortified cereals daily helps increase vitamin B12 concentrations.

In fact, one study showed that when participants ate 1 cup (240 ml) of fortified cereal containing 4.8 mcg (200% of the DV) of vitamin B12 daily for 14 weeks, their vitamin B12 levels increased significantly.

If you choose to use fortified cereal to increase your vitamin B12 intake, make sure to choose a brand low in added sugar and high in fibre or whole grains.

SUMMARY

Cereal fortified with vitamin B12 may also help you increase your vitamin B12 levels. One cup (59 grams) of Malt-O-Meal Raisin Bran provides 62% of the DV.

6. Tuna

Tuna is a commonly consumed fish and great source of nutrients, including protein, vitamins, and minerals.

Tuna contains high concentrations of vitamin B12, especially in the muscles right beneath the skin, which are known as dark muscles.

A 3.5-ounce (100-gram) serving of cooked tuna contains 453% of the DV for the vitamin.

This same serving size also packs a good amount of lean protein, phosphorus, selenium, and vitamins A and B3.

Canned tuna also contains a decent amount of vitamin B12. In fact, a can (165 grams) of light tuna canned in water contains 115% of the DV.

SUMMARY

A 3.5-ounce (100-gram) serving of cooked tuna provides 10.9 mcg of vitamin B12. That's 453% of the DV.

7. Fortified Nutritional Yeast

Nutritional yeast is a good vegan source of protein, vitamins, and minerals.

It's a species of yeast especially grown to be used as food, not as a leavening agent in bread and beer.

Vitamin B12 is not naturally present in nutritional yeast. However, it's commonly fortified, making it a great source of vitamin B12.

As with fortified cereals, the vitamin B12 in nutritional yeast is vegan-friendly because it's synthetically made.

Two tablespoons (15 grams) of nutritional yeast may contain up to 733% of the DV for vitamin B12.

One study added nutritional yeast to the diets of raw-food vegans and found it increased vitamin B12 blood levels and helped reduce blood markers of vitamin B12 deficiency.

SUMMARY

Two tablespoons (15 grams) of nutritional yeast may provide up to 17.6 mcg of vitamin B12. That's 733% of the DV.

8. Trout

Rainbow trout is considered to be one of the healthiest fish.

This freshwater species is a great source of protein, healthy fats, and B vitamins.

A 3.5-ounce (100-gram) serving of trout fillet offers about 312% of the DV for vitamin B12 and 1,171 mg of omega-3 fatty acids.

Experts recommend that the combined daily intake of the omega-3 fatty acids eicosapentaenoic acid (EPA) and docosahexaenoic acid (DHA) should be 250–500 mg.

Trout is also a great source of minerals such as manganese, phosphorus, and selenium.

SUMMARY

> *A 3.5-ounce (100-gram) serving of trout contains 7.5 mcg of vitamin B12. That's 312% of the DV.*

9. Salmon

Salmon is well known for having one of the highest concentrations of omega-3 fatty acids. However, it's also an excellent source of B vitamins.

A half fillet (178 grams) of cooked salmon can pack 208% of the DV for vitamin B12.

The same serving size may also provide 4,123 mg of omega-3 fatty acids.

Alongside its high fat content, salmon offers a high amount of protein, with about 40 grams in a half fillet (178 grams).

SUMMARY

> *A half fillet (178 grams) of cooked salmon offers more than 200% of the DV for vitamin B12.*

10. Fortified Nondairy Milk

Nondairy milk is popular among those who want a nutritious vegan replacement for dairy milk.

While soy, almond, and rice milks are not naturally high in vitamin B12, they are usually fortified, making them an excellent source of this vitamin.

One example is soy milk, which can provide up to 86% of the DV for vitamin B12 in 1 cup (240 ml).

For this reason, fortified non-dairy milks could be a great option for those wanting to increase their vitamin B12 intake and avoid deficiency.

Similarly to the vitamin B12 in other fortified sources, the vitamin B12 in non-dairy milk is synthetically made, so it's vegan-friendly.

SUMMARY

One cup (240 ml) of soy milk contains 2.1 mcg of vitamin B12, or 86% of the DV.

11. Milk And Dairy Products

Milk and dairy products like yogurt and cheese are great sources of protein and several vitamins and minerals, including vitamin B12.

One cup (240 ml) of whole milk supplies 46% of the DV for vitamin B12.

Cheese is also a rich source of vitamin B12. One large slice (22 grams) of Swiss cheese can contain about 28% of the DV.

Full fat plain yogurt can also be a decent source. It has even been shown to help improve vitamin B12 status in people who are deficient in the vitamin.

Interestingly, studies have shown that the body absorbs the vitamin B12 in milk and dairy products better than the vitamin B12 in beef, fish, or eggs.

For example, a study in over 5,000 people showed that dairy was more effective than fish at increasing vitamin B12 levels.

SUMMARY

Dairy is a great source of vitamin B12. One cup of whole or full fat yogurt provides up to 23% of the RDI, and one slice (28 grams) of Swiss cheese contains 16%.

12. Eggs

Eggs are a great source of complete protein and B vitamins, especially B2 and B12.

Two large eggs (100 grams) supply about 46% of the DV for vitamin B12, plus 39% of the DV for vitamin B2.

Research has shown that egg yolks have higher levels of vitamin B12 than egg whites, as well as that the vitamin B12 in egg yolks is easier to absorb. Therefore, it's recommended to eat whole eggs instead of just their whites.

In addition to getting a good dose of vitamin B12, you'll get a healthy amount of vitamin D. Eggs are one of the few foods that naturally contain it, with 11% of the DV in two large eggs.

SUMMARY

Two large eggs (100 grams) contain 1.1 mcg of vitamin B12. That's 46% of the DV.

Should you take vitamin B12 supplements?

Vitamin B12 supplements are recommended for people who are at risk of vitamin B12 deficiency.

Those include older adults, pregnant or breastfeeding women, vegetarians and vegans, individuals with intestinal problems, and those who have had stomach surgery.

As with the vitamin B12 in fortified sources, the vitamin B12 in supplements is synthetically made, so it's vegan-friendly.

Vitamin B12 supplements can be found in many forms. You can swallow, chew, or drink them, or place them under your tongue. Your healthcare provider can also inject you with vitamin B12.

Research has shown that vitamin B12 taken by mouth and muscular injection are equally effective at restoring vitamin B12 levels in people who are deficient in the vitamin.

In fact, a study found that people with low levels of vitamin B12 replenished their stores after 90 days of either supplements or injections of vitamin B12 .

However, not all vitamin B12 deficiency is caused by inadequate dietary intake. It's sometimes caused by lack of intrinsic factor, a protein that is necessary for the efficient absorption of vitamin B12.

Lack of intrinsic factor is most common in older people and usually associated with an autoimmune disease known as pernicious anemia.

The most common treatment for pernicious anemia is lifelong vitamin B12 injections, but small amounts of vitamin B12 are absorbed without intrinsic factor. One review concluded that taking 1,000 mcg daily is an effective alternative to injections.

SUMMARY

> *Vitamin B12 supplements are recommended for people who avoid animal products or with impaired absorption. They can be found in different forms, and dosages range anywhere from 150–2,000 mcg.*

The bottom line

> *Vitamin B12 is a key nutrient that your body needs for many essential functions.*

It can be found in large amounts in animal products, fortified foods, and dietary supplements. Some of the richest sources are liver, beef, sardines, clams, and dairy products.

Whether you want to increase your vitamin stores or prevent deficiency, eating these foods may considerably improve your overall health.

BLOOD-THINNING

Natural blood thinners are substances that reduce the blood's ability to form clots.

Blood clotting is a necessary process, but sometimes the blood can clot too much, leading to complications that can be potentially dangerous.

People who have certain medical conditions, such as congenital heart defects, may require blood-thinning medications to reduce their risk of heart attack or stroke.

It is essential to speak with a doctor before trying these remedies, as they may not work as well as medication and may interfere with some prescription drugs.

Some foods and other substances that may act as natural blood thinners and help reduce the risk of clots include the following list:

1. Turmeric

People have long used the golden spice known as turmeric for culinary and medicinal purposes. The active ingredient in turmeric is curcumin that has anti-inflammatory and blood-thinning or anticoagulant properties.

A study published in 2012 suggests that taking a daily dose of turmeric spice may help people maintain the anticoagulant status of their blood.

People can add turmeric to curries and soups or mix it with hot water to make a comforting tea.

2. Ginger

Ginger is another anti-inflammatory spice that may stop blood clotting. It contains a natural acid called salicylate. Aspirin (acetylsalicylic acid) is a synthetic derivative of salicylate and a potent blood thinner.

To get the anticoagulant effects of natural salicylates, people may want to use fresh or dried ginger regularly in baking, cooking, and juices.

It is unlikely, however, that natural salicylates are as effective as blood-thinning medications.

A 2015 analysis of 10 studies also suggests that ginger's effects on blood clotting are unclear. It indicates that more research is needed to understand the potential blood-thinning properties of ginger fully.

3. Cayenne Peppers

Cayenne peppers are also high in salicylates and can act

as powerful blood-thinning agents.

Cayenne pepper is quite spicy, however, and many people can only tolerate it in small amounts.

Capsules containing cayenne pepper are available in health food stores and online. Other benefits of this spice include lowering blood pressure, increasing circulation, and reducing pain sensations.

4. Vitamin E

Vitamin E reduces blood clotting in a few different ways. These effects depend on the amount of vitamin E that a person takes. The National Institutes of Health's Office of Dietary Supplements suggest that people who are taking blood-thinning drugs should avoid taking large doses of vitamin E.

It is unclear how much vitamin E thins the blood, although it is likely that people would need to take more than 400 International Units (IU) per day. Taking high doses of vitamin E supplements, for example, above 1,500 IU daily, on a long-term basis, may have negative effects.

It may be safer to get vitamin E from foods rather than supplements. Foods that contain vitamin E include:

- almonds
- safflower oil
- sunflower oil
- sunflower seeds

- wheat germ oil
- whole grains

5. Garlic

Besides its often desirable taste in food and cooking, garlic has natural antibiotic and antimicrobial properties.

Some research reports that odourless garlic powder demonstrates antithrombotic activities. An antithrombotic agent is a substance that reduces blood clot formation.

Another review of several studies on garlic suggests that it may thin the blood, although the effects are small and short-lived.

The American Academy of Family Physicians nonetheless recommend that people stop taking high doses of garlic 7 to 10 days before a planned surgery because of its antithrombotic properties.

6. Cassia Cinnamon

Cinnamon contains coumarin, a powerful blood-thinning agent. Warfarin, the most commonly used blood-thinning drug, is derived from coumarin.

Chinese cassia cinnamon contains a much higher coumarin content than Ceylon cinnamon. Taking coumarin-rich cinnamon on a long-term basis can, however, cause liver damage.

It may be best to stick to small amounts of cinnamon in the diet in addition to using other natural blood thinners.

7. Ginkgo Biloba

Practitioners of traditional Chinese medicine have used leaves from the Ginkgo biloba tree for thousands of years. Ginkgo is also a very popular herbal supplement in the United States and Europe. People take it for blood disorders, memory problems, and low energy.

Gingko thins the blood and has fibrinolytic effects, according to some sources. This means it may dissolve blood clots. One study reports that ginkgo extract has similar effects to streptokinase, a drug used to treat blood clots.

The research was, however, done in a laboratory, and not carried out on people or animals. Further research is necessary to see if gingko has the same effects in the human body.

8. Grape Seed Extract

There is some evidence to suggest that grape seed extract may have potential benefits for several heart and blood conditions.

It contains antioxidants that may protect the blood vessels and prevent high blood pressure.

Grape seed extract may also act as a natural blood

thinner. Because of these effects, the National Center for Complementary and Integrative Health suggest that people with blood disorders, those taking blood-thinning medications, and people about to have an operation should not take grape seed extract.

9. Dong Quai

Dong quai, also known as female ginseng, is another traditional Chinese herb that may reduce blood clotting.

Studies on animals report that dong quai significantly increases the length of time it takes blood to clot (prothrombin time).

This effect may result from dong quai's coumarin content, the same substance that makes cinnamon such a potent anticoagulant.

Dong quai is taken orally, and can be consumed as part of a herbal tea or soup.

10. Feverfew

Feverfew is a medicinal herb that comes from the same family as daisies or the Asteraceae family.

People take feverfew for migraines, some digestive disorders, and fever.

Feverfew may also act as a blood thinner by inhibiting the activity of platelets and preventing blood clotting. Feverfew is available in capsule or liquid form.

11. Bromelain

Bromelain is an enzyme that people extract from pineapples. It may be an effective remedy for cardiovascular diseases and high blood pressure.

Research suggests that bromelain can thin the blood, break down blood clots, and reduce clot formation. The enzyme also has anti-inflammatory properties.

Bromelain is available in supplement form from health stores and drug stores.

Takeaway

Many natural substances may reduce clotting to some degree. But natural remedies are unlikely to be as effective as blood-thinning drugs and people at risk of blood clots should not use them instead of prescription medications.

Government authorities do not monitor herbs and supplements as closely as food and drugs. People should research the different brands carefully before buying to ensure they are known for quality and purity.

People taking prescription blood thinners should not use natural remedies without talking to their doctor first.

Even though they are natural, some substances and foods may thin the blood too much, especially when taken in conjunction with medications. This can increase the risk of bleeding.

While people can usually consume foods with potential blood-thinning properties safely in reasonable amounts, it is essential to speak to a doctor before trying herbal remedies, such as dong quai and grape seed extract.

Some of these products should not be taken alongside blood thinning medication.

ABOUT THE AUTHOR

Kenneth Milkas

The author hails from the hilly region of 'The Nilgiris' from the Southern India. He's passionate on sharing important and sensible information to others for their benefit. He's a successful banker. Very diplomatic in nature. He's been creative and has been sharing motivational articles to students, teens and institutions through his weekly publications "My Life". He's spiritually inclined. Hailing from a beautiful family and is passionate on building lasting relationships. His books cover topics that impact our daily lives. He aims to support charities from the sale of his books.

BOOKS BY THIS AUTHOR

Blissful Married Life

Marriage is not easy and it is not always "fun.". It's a rollercoaster ride. No- matter how hard you try to prove you are "right," to keep a marriage strong, you might have to admit that you are "wrong." Marriage is not finding the perfect partner but becoming one. Fights need to be fair and with dignity and respect. The first to forgive is always great. "Marriage" means that this is forever, no matter how sick you are, there is someone who will support you and love you no matter what. Marriage also means that in every battle you face, there is someone who takes it as personally as you do. The imperfect two become one.

Motivational Quotes For The Professional Sales Person

Any successful business leader will testify to the fact that sales are the lifeblood of any organisation. A Sales Person faces obstacles, overcomes hurdles, counters challenges to win customers. Therefore, a sales person needs encouragement, self- motivation and inspiration to be consistent in sales. Motivation is one of the most important components of sustained sales success over time. Without the income and revenue generated by consistent sales, a company will fail to achieve the growth and expansion required to survive in the harsh conditions of today's economy; a good reason if ever there was one to invest some time and effort into developing an efficient and competent sales team. Motivated sales teams enjoy their work more and do their work better, resulting in a healthier bottom line. Here are over 500 motivational quotes to motivate your salesforce; to keep them happy and productive.

Mary The Mother Of Jesus

Mary was Chosen by God himself to be the mother of his only begotten Son, Jesus. She bore the son of God in her womb and groomed him so well as per the will of the heavenly father. Mary, the mother of Jesus, commonly referred to as Mary, Mother of God, Saint Mary, Virgin Mary and Blessed Virgin Mary, is one of the most admired figures in Scripture and considered by many to be the greatest of all Christian saints. She was a willing servant who trusted God and obeyed His call. While her life held great honour, her calling also required great suffering. Though there was joy in motherhood, there was great pain in the privilege of being the mother of the Messiah. Despite these things, she responded to God with great obedience and submission to His plan. Her life never robbed Jesus of His glory, for her mission was to witness the glory of the Son of God. Here are fascinating facts about Mary, Mother of Jesus that everyone should know.

The Book Of Proverbs

The Book of Proverbs can make to your spiritual life. Proverbs is a book that is concerned with the development and assessment of godly character. No book in all the Bible is more devoted to the development of godly character than Proverbs. whether you believe in the Bible or not, the book of Proverbs has a wealth of wisdom for anyone who is listening, so I encourage you to read this article and hopefully gather a few nuggets from this book. The book's superscription, "The proverbs of Solomon. . . ," is not to say that it as a whole or even individual proverbs should be credited to King Solomon, for scholarly examination discloses that it contains seven collections of wisdom materials (mostly short sayings) from a wide variety of periods, all after Solomon's time. And there is no greater need in the Christian community today than for the kind of character Proverbs extols.

Promises Of God

God speaks to his people through various people, known and unknown to them. His voice is loud and clear. His words comfort us, heals us, fills us with hope, protects us, gives us courage and blesses us. The Son of God, Lord Jesus Christ has demonstrated to us his abounding love by dying for us on the cross for our sins. His words are an inspiration for all of us to travel in the right direction towards eternal life. The Bible is filled with the promises of God. From Genesis to Revelation we read of normal people that received the promises of God. These promises are sealed by the highest authority, God's word. In

Hebrews 6:13 it says, "For when God made a promise to Abraham, since he had no one greater by whom to swear, he swore by himself." It's important that Christians know the Word of God and write it on their hearts. In times of trouble, stress, and despair, it is the God's promises that give us hope. The scriptures remind us that with our eyes fixed on Christ we can weather any storm that comes our way. Biblical stories assure us that God will never abandon us and that He will always welcome us back into His loving arms. Don't let the devil steal your joy and strength in the Lord. Memorize, print, or save this link so that you can always find these promises when you need them the most. This book is a collection of the words of hope from every book of the Holy Bible.

Inspirations For A Wonderful Life

Life offers great opportunity for learning. We often focus on complex issues, but seldom do we realize that we can get inspired from simple things in life. We learn from everything and from every moment that comes in to our life. We become special if we understand, what life's circumstances teach us. This book provides us insight in to those little things that can influence us positively.
Everyone longs to be healthy and happy. Balanced living means considering all aspects of your life: relationships, work, fitness and health, and emotional well-being.
So, recharge your body physically and mentally and make the commitment to enjoy some "you time" every day. Being happy gives you a better outlook on life, so you're more prepared to tackle your tasks. Make time to take care of yourself and indulge in creative outlets you enjoy to help with stress reduction. This book provides

information on various important topics to inspire us to live a wonderful life.